Aging and the
Perception of Speech

Aging and the Perception of Speech is a volume in the PERSPECTIVES IN AUDIOLOGY SERIES—Lyle L. Lloyd, series editor. Other volumes in the series include:

Published:

Communicating with Deaf People: A Resource Manual for Teachers and Students of American Sign Language by Harry W. Hoemann, Ph.D.

Language Development and Intervention with the Hearing Impaired by Richard R. Kretschmer, Jr., Ed.D., and Laura W. Kretschmer, Ed.D.

Noise and Audiology edited by David M. Lipscomb, Ph.D.

The Sounds of Speech Communication: A Primer of Acoustic Phonetics and Speech Perception by J. M. Pickett, Ph.D.

Supervision in Audiology by Judith A. Rassi, M.A.

Hearing Assessment edited by William F. Rintelmann, Ph.D.

Auditory Management of Hearing-Impaired Children: Principles and Prerequisites for Intervention edited by Mark Ross, Ph.D., and Thomas G. Giolas, Ph.D.

Introduction to Aural Rehabilitation edited by Ronald L. Schow, Ph.D., and Michael A. Nerbonne, Ph.D.

Acoustical Factors Affecting Hearing Aid Performance edited by Gerald A. Studebaker, Ph.D., and Irving Hochberg, Ph.D.

American Sign Language and Sign Systems by Ronnie Bring Wilbur, Ph.D.

In preparation:

Principles of Speech Audiometry edited by Dan F. Konkle, Ph.D., and William F. Rintelmann, Ph.D.

Forensic Audiology edited by Marc B. Kramer, Ph.D., and Joan M. Armbruster, M.S.

Acoustic Amplification: A Unified Treatment by Harry Levitt, Ph.D.

The Development of Special Auditory Testing: A Book of Readings edited by Jay Sanders, Jr., Ph.D., and M. Richard Navarro, Ph.D.

Publisher's Note

Perspectives in Audiology is a carefully planned series of clinically oriented and basic science textbooks. The series is enriched by contributions from leading specialists in audiology and allied disciplines. Because technical language and terminology in these disciplines are constantly being refined and sometimes vary, this series has been edited as far as possible for consistency of style in conformity with current majority usage as set forth by the American Speech-Language-Hearing Association, the *Publication Manual of the American Psychological Association,* and The University of Chicago's *A Manual of Style.* University Park Press and the series editors and authors welcome readers' comments about individual volumes in the series or the series concept as a whole in the interest of making **Perspectives in Audiology** as useful as possible to students, teachers, clinicians, and scientists.

A Volume in the Perspectives in Audiology Series

AGING AND THE PERCEPTION OF SPEECH

by
Moe Bergman, Ed.D.
Professor
School for Communication Disorders
Sackler School of Medicine
Tel-Aviv University
and
Professor Emeritus
Hunter College of the City University of New York

University Park Press
Baltimore

UNIVERSITY PARK PRESS
International Publishers in Science, Medicine, and Education
233 East Redwood Street
Baltimore, Maryland 21202

Composed by University Park Press, Typesetting Division.
Manufactured in the United States of America by The Maple Press Company.

Illustrations by Jean Zéboulon,
Sackler School of Medicine, Tel-Aviv University.

Library of Congress Cataloging in Publication Data
Bergman, Moe.
Aging and the perception of speech. (Perspectives in audiology series)
Bibliography: p.   Includes indexes.
1. Presbycusis. 2. Speech perception. 3. Aging.
I. Title. II. Series. [DNLM: 1. Speech perception—In old age. WL705 B499a]
RF291.5.A35B47   618.97'78   80-11512
ISBN 0-8391-1589-X

To Hannah and Jay

CONTENTS

PREFACE TO PERSPECTIVES IN AUDIOLOGY

Audiology is a young, vibrant, dynamic field. Its lineage can be traced to the fields of education, medicine, physics, and psychology in the nineteenth century and the emergence of speech pathology in the first half of this century. The term *audiology*, meaning the science of hearing, was coined by Raymond Carhart in 1945. Since then, its definition has expanded to include its professional nature. Audiology is the profession that provides knowledge and service in the areas of human hearing and, more broadly, human communication and its disorders. Audiology is also a major area of study in the professional preparation of speech pathologists, speech and hearing scientists, teachers of the hearing impaired, and otologists.

Perspectives in Audiology is the first series of books designed to cover the major areas of study in audiology. The interdisciplinary nature of the field is reflected by the scope of the volumes in this series. The volumes (see p. ii) include both clinically oriented and basic science texts. The series consists of topic-specific textbooks designed to meet the needs of today's advanced level student and of focal references for practicing audiologists and specialists in many related fields.

The **Perspectives in Audiology** series offers several advantages not usually found in other texts, but purposely featured in this series to increase the practical value of the books for practitioners and researchers, as well as for students and teachers.

1. Every volume includes thorough discussion of relevant clinical and/or research papers on each topic.
2. Most volumes are organized in an educational format to serve as the main text or as one of the main texts for graduate and advanced undergraduate students in courses on audiology and/or other studies concerned with human communication and its disorders.
3. Unlike ordinary texts, **Perspectives in Audiology** volumes will retain their professional reference value as focal reference sources for practitioners and researchers in career work long after completion of their studies.
4. Each volume serves as a rich source of authoritative, up-to-date information and valuable reviews for specialists in many fields, such as administration, audiology, early childhood studies, linguistics, otology, psychology, pediatrics, public health, special education, speech pathology, and/or speech and hearing science.

Aging has become one of the nation's major health and social issues. Audiologists and others concerned with human communication and its disorders are confronted with many practical problems as a result of the aging process. This timely volume on *Aging and the Perception of Speech* provides the practicing audiologist and others concerned with the topic of aging and perception of speech with a major collection of research spearheaded by one of the men responsible for the development of audiology as a profession. This book represents, as do many of the volumes in the **Perspectives in Audiology** series, a combination of basic research and practical clinical considerations. However, the volume does deviate from most of the other works in the series in that it focuses primarily on the work of one investigator and his close colleagues.

Professor Bergman's research provides the first major work on the topic of aging and speech perception. As such, it serves as a valuable reference for students in training and practicing professionals.

Lyle L. Lloyd, Ph.D.
Chairman and Professor of Special Education
Professor of Audiology and Speech Sciences
Purdue University

PREFACE

Some years ago, when I was spending a sabbatical year in Israel, I attended a lecture by another visiting American, the eminent gerontologist Nathan W. Shock. I had not expected to take lecture notes on that pleasantly warm evening, but as I listened I was moved to fish some scraps of paper out of my pocket and to jot down some of the central themes of that memorable talk by the incoming President of the International Association of Gerontology. Two quotes in my yellowing notes stood out as I undertook to write this book on a relatively neglected aspect of aging behavior: "To prolong longevity is *not* a worthy goal of gerontology. To reduce the detrimental effects of aging *is* very much a worthwhile goal." And the most instructive dictum for those who venture into the mysteries of aging: "To study aging we cannot study only old people, we must study the whole lifespan."

The first of these expressions was and remains a sobering reminder that the ultimate purpose of our studies must be the improvement of the quality of life for a large segment of our population.

We had already been involved in trying to satisfy Shock's second dictum by collecting field data on the speech understanding of adults from 20 through 90 years of age. Those studies, begun in 1965 in the United States, and subsequent investigations in Israel since early 1975 led to the development of this book.

There is now an explosion of research and publication in diverse aspects of gerontology. This is not surprising since we are suddenly finding so many middle age and older persons among us. Startled responses to this reality are not limited to professional workers, as witness the stampede of legislators voting their newfound concerns for their "senior" constituencies. (Note the U.S. House of Representatives vote of 359 to 4 for a bill extending the mandatory retirement age in private industry and removing it altogether for federal employees.) They and we are reminded repeatedly in articles in the mass media, as well as in the professional literature, that the proportions of the different segments in our population are shifting dramatically toward increased age. In countries where the birth rate is dropping, such as the United States, it is expected that persons above 55 years of age, who now make up just under 20% of the population, will constitute over 27% after the turn of the century, and the under-20 years of age proportion will fall from over 33% to about even with that of the over-55 group. The median age in the United States, which is now about 28, will reach 35 by the year 2000 and will rise to near 40, 30 years later ("The Graying of America," 1977, *Newsweek,* February 28).

It is apparent that increasing numbers of citizens of middle and later ages will continue to have important roles in major functions of our society. This places additional stress on the need for communicative efficiency, particularly for those for whom today's communication conditions and systems are relatively inappropriate for their own changing physiologic and psychologic systems. It is for this reason that the emphasis in this book is on the important middle, highly productive years, as well as on the later periods of life.

It is hoped that the following reports and discussions on the understanding of speech under a variety of listening conditions and variables in the listener himself will be useful to our colleagues in gerontology, psychology, communications, and social work as well as to those who are in audiology and otology. Perhaps also our standards for communication systems, which have often been based upon the superior auditory and perceptual abilities of young adults, will be adjusted in accordance with the emerging realities of the shifting age distribution in our society.

ACKNOWLEDGMENTS

It is clear that our work, in common with most research, evolved from the previous insights and reports of others. Among the many whose pioneering efforts were invaluable to our investigations and to the formulations included in this book are the following, who I feel were particularly influential on my own thinking about aging audition. Dr. Harold Schuknecht of the Harvard University Medical School and his colleagues have neatly organized our knowledge about presbycusis and its anatomical and physiological bases. Dr. Cornelius P. Goetzinger, of the University of Kansas Medical School, has persistently pursued the threads of age-related decline in the perception of speech. For me, a germinal paper on the widespread age-related changes in the entire auditory mechanism was that published in 1962 by Dr. Ronald Hinchcliffe, of the Institute of Otology in London. For the burgeoning application of a variety of auditory measures of central function, we must acknowledge the generative reports by Dr. Ettore Bocca and his colleagues in Italy.

Our own investigations, many of which are reported here, were the result of joint efforts with colleagues and university students in the United States and Israel. While much of our work was carried out as academic and university-based laboratory research, invaluable early support in the United States (1965–1968) was provided by the National Institute of Child Health and Human Development and in Israel by the Ministry of Absorption.

In our early uncertainties about how to attack the problems of aging auditory behavior, we turned to one for whom we had an awesome respect, Dr. J. Donald Harris, of the Submarine Medical Research Laboratory at Groton, Connecticut. Dr. Harris, with his incomparable clarity, made major contributions in ideas and test materials at the beginning of our American studies. Another great colleague whose ideas were seminal to our research design was the late Grant Fairbanks, and our shaky entrance into the mysteries of population sampling was guided by the knowledgeable counsel of Dr. Gordon Fifer of Hunter College of the City University of New York.

Colleagues at the City University of New York Communication Sciences Laboratory who contributed to this work were Professor Harry Levitt, who unstintingly gives so much of his energy to so many, Harvey Stromberg and Ron Slosberg, who calmly and cheerfully instructed the computer to spew out so much pertinent data, and Carole Mayer, part of whose study on the interference by New York City noises of the speech perception of aging city dwellers is summarized here.

My research colleagues in our first American studies at the Parkchester, Bronx, New York housing project were Elliott Millner, who conceived the idea of the project at that development, Vera Gruber Blumenfeld, Maris K. Margulies, and Marc B. Kramer.

Audiology students at Hunter College of the City University of New York whom I was honored to direct in their academic degree-related research and whose results are included in this book are Debra Cascardo, Barbara Dash, Alberta Hall, Susan Kaen, Lily Klein Karsai, Edward Kirsh, Janice Klazkin, Alisa Levine Ludwig, and Ruth Ann Voigt.

In Israel, I enjoyed the close cooperation and devoted field work of Nadia Fogel for the major field study reported here and was able to mount a variety of studies through the efforts of the following students at our School for Communication Disorders of the Tel-Aviv University: Rachel Anafi, Rina Biran, Yechiella Bistriski, Bilha Bramson, Chaia Burger, Leora Chavkin, Ilana Cohen, Ronit

Goshen, Naomi DeWalt, Nahama Halpern, Hagit Hofi, Ruth Lev, Anath Mermelstein, Zvia Muttath, Livia Pasternak, Sima Rejwan, and Rachel Shemesh. Mrs. Yael Frank, our faculty phonetician, was of great help in analyzing the recorded voices of talkers used in several of our studies.

I am grateful to Jean Zéboulon for his very concise and attractive illustrations and to Stella Padeh for her careful typing of the manuscript.

Above all I want to acknowledge my humble gratitude to the companion and supporter of the major part of my life, my wife Hannah, whose contributions not only to this book but to all that preceded it are too infinitudinal even to grasp.

My final acknowledgment is to our son Jay, from whose emergence as a scholar and teacher I have drawn renewed inspiration.

Aging and the
Perception of Speech

CHAPTER 1

INTRODUCTION
The Assessment
of Auditory Behavior

CONTENTS

> We may as well face squarely the losses we risk by surviving early maturity
> and middle age and by understanding these hazards try to minimize them.
>
> G. A. Talland (1968, p. ix)

The understanding of spoken communication is a fundamental need for man in his association with other humans. Although acquiring such understanding is deceptively easy for the infant and young child, it is built on enormously complex processes, involving many possibilities for failure. It is heavily dependent first upon the reception and differentiation of individual sounds by the ear mechanism and then upon the processing of the resultant product in the brain. Thus a serious hearing or central auditory system disorder in young children can frustrate the establishment of the basic linguistic blocks for spoken communication and learning. Much thought and effort have been devoted to the early discovery and treatment of childhood deafness and, more recently, of childhood receptive language disorders.

Considerably less attention has been focused upon the decline of speech perception that often accompanies aging.

As in the development of speech understanding in childhood, age-related decline involves a complex interaction of the peripheral and central auditory systems. Since the perception of speech first requires appropriate function of the peripheral hearing mechanism, studies of the decline in the ear's sensitivity, with age, have been conducted in the United States and elsewhere since the first quarter of this century, using the pure tone audiometer. Such studies, carried out mostly in urban areas,

1

are now being augmented by investigators who are visiting remote populations in various corners of the world.

In a significant departure from the pure tone audiometer approach to aging audition, recent investigations have focused increasingly upon the decrement in the understanding of speech, thus elevating the anatomical levels of interest from the end organ of hearing to the auditory pathways to the brain, and to the complex functions of the brain itself. In a further shift of emphasis, the clinical tests of hearing for isolated words heard under carefully controlled ideal listening conditions are being discarded as inappropriate to the study of age-related changes of hearing for speech under a realistic variety of listening conditions by nonclinic persons in favor of newer measures. It is in the findings of such a sampling of actual auditory function under conditions resembling activities of daily living that the socially disturbing effects are expected to be seen. These effects may be viewed as a gradual and apparently continuous reduction, for many aging adults, in the kind and amount of information that the speech of others provides, resulting in a "disuse atrophy" of intellectual and emotional life. Such reduction of input may occur because of failing hearing or the even more pervasive central changes resulting in the decrease of understanding heard through electronic transmission or in the presence of competing noise. It is reasonable to suspect a significant link between the decline in the stimulation that speech provides and fading social interaction leading to dullness in the later years for so many.

The ultimate purpose of studies of aging behavior must be, of course, as our opening quote states so succinctly, the minimizing of the effects of the undesirable changes. Eventually, a book of this sort may be structured in three major parts: 1) description of the phenomena of aging speech perception, 2) analysis of the physiological and psychological factors in the listener that account for the altered behavior, and 3) application of the knowledge for the prevention or remediation (i.e., compensation) of the changes. Unfortunately, ability to treat all three of these topics satisfactorily at present is severely limited because of lack of sufficient research findings. The stimulus for the preparation of this book was the development of experimental information accumulated by myself and my students and colleagues over a period of approximately 13 years in the United States and Israel primarily in two languages, English and Hebrew. Such information can be classed essentially under part 1 above, description. This seems to follow the chronology of gerontological reports in other fields as well.

In short, before we can meet the problems of declining communicative functioning in aging persons, we must learn specifically what changes in auditory skills and performance tend to occur with aging; then we can turn our attention to how we might alter the conditions of the older listener's interaction with his communicating environment in order to reduce the disabling effects. The great need for this is stated soberly by Weinberg (1972), writing on the key role played by perception in providing an individual with information from his environment and the importance of this to his psychological functions, such as memory, judgment, and anticipation: "The gradual isolation of the aging organism into a state of aloneness is the great tragedy of aging."

THE ASSESSMENT OF AUDITORY BEHAVIOR

This book is concerned primarily with the uniquely human aspect of auditory behavior, the understanding of speech. The term *auditory behavior* implies far greater complexity than was encompassed by the earlier interest of ear and hearing specialists in sensitivity for audiometric tones. For the understanding of speech it suggests at least a tripodal construct built upon: 1) hearing (a peripheral attribute), 2) listening (probably a middle level central function), and 3) auding (listening with comprehension). Each of these is influenced, in turn, by internal factors of the listener himself, by external conditions of the message and its physical environment, and by the linguistic concurrence between the talker and the listener.

How shall we approach an evaluation of the success or failure of such a multidimensional process? As in so many problem-solving situations, there is a choice of various alternatives, each yielding useful, if dissimilar, insights. The seven approaches suggested here are not meant to be exhaustive or mutually exclusive.

The Psychoacoustic and Phonemic Perception Approach

There is a rich literature reporting sophisticated experiments on the perception and neural encoding of the physical aspects of acoustic signals, specifically, their frequency, amplitude, and time characteristics. Research on the response of the organism ("psycho-") to sound ("-acoustic") ranges from absolute sensitivity (the mechanisms of the perception and differentiation of single pitches and combinations of tones) to masking effects of competing sounds, through the discrimination of speech phonemes. At best, however, the reception and differentiation of acoustic signals and their transmission as appropriate neural patterns, and even phoneme discriminations, are only *contributors* to the useful perception of the speech message. In a conservative statement of this, Hirsh (1967) cautioned that we will not be able to evaluate hearing for speech from an analysis of "the various psychoacoustic subabilities that seem to underlie" speech perception. In the light of the great concentration of experimental effort invested in the phenomena of phoneme perception, it is sobering to consider the remarks in a letter to the editor of the *Journal of the Acoustical Society of America* by J. R. Pierce (1969) who, in a quasi-philosophical discussion of the feasibility of machine recognition of speech, stated the problem clearly:

> There are strong reasons for believing that spoken English is, in general, simply not recognizable phoneme by phoneme or word by word, and that people recognize utterances, not because they hear the phonetic features of the words distinctly, but because they have a general sense of what a conversation is about and are able to guess what has been said.

It is thus the implied *central* functions of speech perception that beckon those who would investigate age-related changes. This is apparently true for other sensory perceptions as well, namely, the observation for vision: "Measures of static acuity have limited value in predicting the ability of older persons to detect details in moving targets" (Fozard et al., 1977). The understanding of speech involves such listener-to-listener variables as operate in the *patterning* of phonemic and prosodic information (intonation, stress, temporal relationships, etc.) and in such psychological phenomena as short-term memory, expectancy, selective and sustained attention, and synthesis.

The Site-of-Lesion Approach

In line with the burst of interest, in audiology, in using tests of varying complexity and technology to locate central vs. peripheral auditory pathology, we might follow the example of A. R. Luria (1970, 1973) (Figure 1.1), who conceived of the brain as being divided into three blocks, the first of which encompasses the reticular alerting system (RAS), controls wakefulness, and regulates the energy tone of the cortex. To his second block, which is posterior to the central sulcus and the temporal lobe, Luria assigned a hierarchical organization of three zones, which are responsible for specified phases of information processing. The frontal lobes, which form his third block, he linked to the RAS in the regulation of attention and concentration. Luria's extensive experience with patients with brain injuries led him to believe that specific cortical centers exist for such discrete perceptual functions as spatiality (e.g., recognition of the form of the letter *s*) and sequentiality (e.g., *c a t,* in that order). Present advances in neuroaudiology—instrumental (Sohmer and Feinmesser, 1973), behavioral (Bergman, Hirsch, and Najenson, 1977; Keith, 1977), and combined instrumental and behavioral (Lynn and Gilroy, 1977)— give promise of relating subtle changes in auditory perception to alterations in the function of specified areas of the central auditory nervous system (CANS). Such diagnostic approaches are predicated on the premise that the demonstrated dysfunction is localized in one or more identifiable areas of the CANS. Although such a premise should be considered, it is still not clear how specific or how general are the neurophysiological changes accompanying aging that might be involved in altered perception of speech.

The Linguistic-Specificity Approach

Related to the topographical basis of the site-of-lesion approach is the work of those who have pursued the remarkable revelations by Broadbent (1954) and Kimura (1961) that one-half of the brain (the left hemisphere in most of us) is dominant in the understanding of speech. Shankweiler and Studdert-Kennedy (1967) refined this concept further by demonstrating that the important linguistic elements of speech, namely, the consonants, account for this hemispheric specialization. As a first approximation, it is reasonable to suppose that there are specialized brain areas for applying the rules of grammar (the syntax) to the perception of speech messages.

There is some evidence of a close relationship between our expressive language function and our perception of language. Luria (1970) noted that when we write from dictation we often silently articulate the words by mouth, and children repeat a dictated word to themselves before writing it. Luria supported this relationship with the report that damage to the expressive areas of the brain results in the confusion of phonemes that are heard.

Liberman (1957) has proposed that there is an important link between the expressive activity of the listener and his perception of speech.

It seems reasonable to expect further advances of this sort in which the processing of various aspects of speech will be found to be related to specific locations or functions of the central system. Such advances can be expected to aid the understanding of the details of aging changes related to the subprocesses of speech perception.

The Semantic-Probability Approach

A vital element in the understanding of a message is discerning its meaning. Although obvious, this aspect has been almost entirely neglected in measures of speech perception. Given the same message, immersed in the same acoustic environment, and received by a similar peripheral hearing system, what differences in the cognitive abilities of different listeners account for their relative success in understanding it?

A tentative approach to such a measure is the recent introduction of the Speech Perception in Noise (SPIN) test (Kalikow, Stevens, and El-

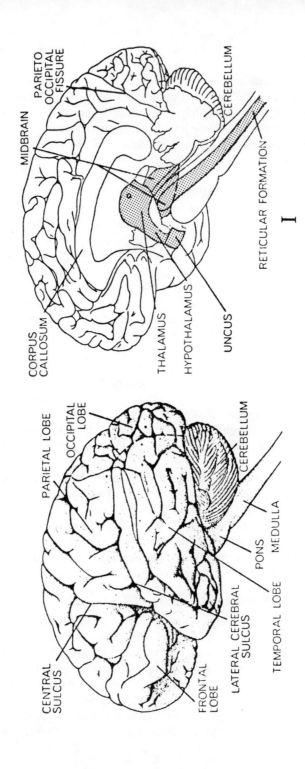

CENTRAL SULCUS

PARIETAL LOBE

OCCIPITAL LOBE

CEREBELLUM

PONS

MEDULLA

TEMPORAL LOBE

LATERAL CEREBRAL SULCUS

FRONTAL LOBE

MIDBRAIN

PARIETO OCCIPITAL FISSURE

CEREBELLUM

RETICULAR FORMATION

UNCUS

HYPOTHALAMUS

THALAMUS

CORPUS CALLOSUM

I

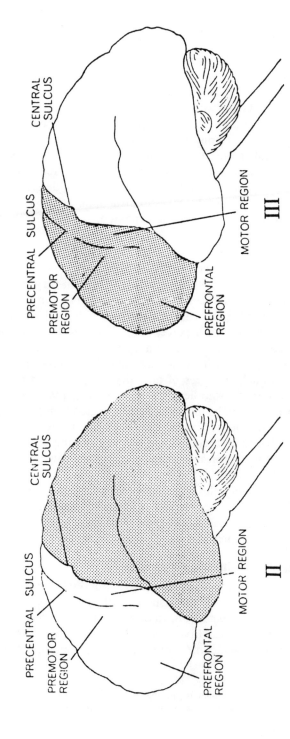

Figure 1.1. Luria's formulation of the human brain's three fundamental blocks, as discussed in the text. The gross anatomy is depicted at upper left. (From A. R. Luria, 1970, "The Functional Organization of the Brain," *Scientific American*, March, p. 67. Copyright © 1970 by Scientific American, Inc. All rights reserved.)

7

liott, 1977), in which the listener's ability to utilize the syntactic and semantic information of a sentence to recognize its final (test) word is assessed. In this test each of the test words is presented twice, once without contextual cues and once with such cues. The application of this test to studies of aging perception and first results are discussed in Chapter 8.

The listener is always at a disadvantage with respect to the talker. For example, when the talker uses a homophone,[1] the listener must apply a probability test. It is reasonable to conclude, from the increasing spread of performance among adults of advancing age in the understanding of degraded speech messages, that this measurement approach holds considerable promise that has too long been unexploited.

The Psychological Approach

Understanding a spoken message usually requires such listener functions as attention and memory as well as cognition. These in turn are intertwined with degrees of alertness, states of well-being, and emotion (mood). It is pertinent to inquire what role such psychological factors play in age-related changes in speech perception. What are the age-related changes in vigilance, or the relative constancy of performance in this activity? (A common experience in audiology clinics is the relative instability of speech discrimination scores of an older person who is tested at more than one test session.) Another challenging point is the oft-reported tendency of older persons to be more rigid in their set. We might ask, for example, how ready are they to track the shifts of message focus? Again, since aging is reported to be accompanied by deterioration of aspects of memory, how does this factor affect the perception of low-redundancy spoken messages?

The psychological dynamics of aging listeners have not yet received structured attention, despite the existence of a wealth of published material in works on gerontology. It would seem that this is a fertile area for dedicated research and clinical effort.

The Hierarchical, Signal-Alteration Approach

The perception of speech has been described as a progressive process (theoretically, although it is possible that aspects of the process occur essentially simultaneously) from detection, to discrimination, to recognition, and finally to comprehension (Hirsh, 1967). This might be expanded to include detailed steps in the hierarchy of the speech perception process as follows:

---

[1]Words, either similar or dissimilar in spelling, that sound alike but have different meanings. An example is the word *land:* verb form—to land on one's feet; noun form—the land under one's feet.

I.   Reception
    A.   Threshold sensitivity for various stimuli
    B.   Accuracy of encoding
        1.   Peripheral encoding
            a.   intensity
            b.   frequency
            c.   time
        2.   Neural patterning, e.g., of speech sounds, masking effects
II. Neural transmission and fusion
    A.   Predecussation
    B.   Postdecussation
III. Processing
    A.   Recognition of patterns
        1.   Segmental
        2.   Suprasegmental (loudness, pitch, timbre, intonation, pause, stress, rhythm)
    B.   Short-term memory
        1.   Auditory memory span
        2.   Auditory sequential memory
    C.   Auditory figure-ground discrimination
    D.   Auditory synthesis (e.g., sound blending)
    E.   Linguistic processing: syntactic, semantic
    F.   Multimodal integration (i.e., intersensory integration, for example, visual-auditory)

Such a list of steps in the process suggests the possible usefulness of employing graded sets of test tasks, each presumably exposing weaknesses in one or more stages of the process. For example, since discrimination requires perception of the basic acoustic attributes of frequency, amplitude, and time, these aspects can be manipulated, separately or in combination. This, of course, is not a novel idea, French and Steinberg (1947) (among others) having developed data on the influence of frequency distortion on the understanding of speech. The application of such frequency distortion, amplitude distortion (e.g., peak clipping), and temporal alterations to the study of aging phenomena, however, is still in its earliest stages. The effects of some aspects of these and other signal alterations are discussed in this book.

The Functional Profile Approach

An appealing way to examine a person's behavior comprehensively is to construct a descriptive profile embracing at least the main aspects of that person's activities of daily living. Thus we might list prime listening situations and needs and assign a relative rating to performance in each. We might either construct tests for each of these or ask the subject to complete self-assessment questionnaires, or use both approaches. The use of self-assessment scales in a study of aging speech perception was reported by Blumenfeld, Bergman, and Millner (1969), but it seems little has been reported so far on the construction of the suggested functional profile as a description of aging perception of speech.

SUMMARY

It is apparent that the understanding of age-related changes in the perception of speech under various conditions may be approached in many ways. Some of these have been attempted in the studies reported in this book. It is clear that there are almost limitless possibilities for extended and more innovative research in this, the first step toward the goal of improving the quality of life for aging adults through optimum spoken communication.

CHAPTER 2

AGING AND SENSORY PERCEPTION

CONTENTS

THE PROCESSES OF AGING

Published material and professional activity in the area of aging generally fall into one of three broad categories: *biological* aging, which is concerned with the state of the individual's organ systems as an indicator of his potential life-span; *psychological* or *behavioral* aging, which encompasses such aspects of adaptive functioning as intelligence, memory, learning, and skills as well as feelings, emotions, attention, and motivation; and *social* aging, in which an individual's habits and roles are compared to those of other members of his group or society, that is, to their social norms or values.

There appear to be several assumptions about the processes of aging. One holds that at some point in adulthood the level of function reaches its maximum, after which decrement occurs, proceeding either linearly or at an accelerating rate. Examples of the latter, particularly involving the seventh decade of life, are included in later chapters, particularly Chapters 7, 8, and 9. Another theory of aging points to measures like intelligence and argues that once maturity is reached, adult behavior remains stable. An encouraging construct predicts age-related decrements after maximum function has been reached, but argues that such changes may be remediated by altering the environment. This, of course, is most compatible with attempts at constructive intervention.

An interesting additional aspect of the mechanisms of aging is that of the relative roles of genetic factors and deleterious environmental influences. This is of significant importance to the understanding of auditory behavior because it is increasingly evident that the function of the peripheral hearing mechanism is determined by both, whereas the relationships to central message processing function are still largely unexplored.

In recent literature on the psychology of aging the emphasis is on *functional* age in contrast to earlier concentration on chronologically

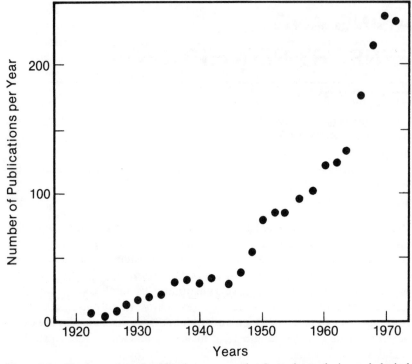

Figure 2.1.   Yearly number of publications, averaged at 2-year intervals, in psychological gerontology. (From K. F. Riegel in J. E. Birren and K. W. Schaie (eds.), *Handbook of the Psychology of Aging,* p. 93, © 1977 by Litton Educational Publishing, Inc. Reprinted by permission of Van Nostrand Reinhold Co., New York.)

related peripheral changes. Judgments of functional age therefore are generally based on performance tests.

This book is concerned with the hearing and understanding of speech, and therefore relates most closely to the general topic of behavioral aging. Since no major aspect of aging behavior is independent of the other two, the efficiency of spoken communication depends upon the biological state of the aging person as well as his need for and use of communication skills as a vital social instrument.

As in the discipline of psychology, workers in the area of interpersonal spoken communication have been much interested in the *developmental* changes that occur in the maturing child, partly because such changes occur quite rapidly—a convenience for the researcher. Age-related behavioral changes of the declining end of the life-span, however, have only relatively recently attracted research and publication interest. An informative review of the long, slow start and recent surge of interest in psychological gerontology, for example, is provided by Riegel (1977) and is illustrated in Figure 2.1. Major topics of published articles in that field were concerned with intelligence, memory, health, personality, perceptual and motor skills, language functions (e.g., reading, vocabulary, writing speed), sexual attitudes, social aspects, problem-solving (e.g., rigidity tests), attitudes tests (e.g., toward life, retirement, and family), and physical and psychiatric measures.

Publication activity in what might be referred to as communicative gerontology is now similar to that between 1920 and 1930 in psychological gerontology.

Added to the late start in the development of studies has been the tendency, in audiology, to confuse aging behavior with behavior of *old* persons only. This is currently yielding to the conviction that studies of aging should be concerned with the entire life-span.

Aging does not necessarily involve decline in all behavioral functions. There is some evidence, for example (Granick and Birren, 1969), that persons who survive into their 80s show no significant decline in intellectual vigor and capabilities and in fact show some increases on the vocabulary and picture arrangement subtests of the Wechsler Adult Intelligence Scale (WAIS). Aging follows different timetables in each person. A persistent observation in studies of age-related behavior is the great range of performance among older *Ss,* as indicated by the tendency for variances around statistical means to be larger than for younger groups. Evidence of this in studies of speech perception is presented in Chapter 10.

Aging encompasses diverse changes in the human organism—physiological, psychological, and social—ranging from molecular aspects of each of these to complex, multi-tiered functions. Small-unit changes, e.g., detailed peripheral alterations in a sense organ like the ear or the eye, are relatively universal with aging. Significant decrement of actual function, however, apparently results from the complex interaction between the peripheral organ and various areas of the central nervous system (CNS) and often cannot be predicted from the peripheral changes alone. In muscular work, for example, the decrements in individual organ systems are less than those in total performance. Shock (1977) concluded that this "may well be a reflection of impaired integrative functions at the neural and integrative levels."

Expositions of nervous system changes with aging frequently refer to electroencephalography (EEG) findings. For example, it has been reported that normal elderly persons frequently show bursts of slow waves (1–7 per sec) with high amplitude (Marsh and Thompson, 1977). About 75% of these bursts of focal slowing occur in the left hemisphere, mostly over the anterior temporal region. It is interesting to note that this is the presumed critical area for linguistic activity. There is apparently some possibility, however, that the actual focus of these slow bursts, although seen over the temporal area, may originate elsewhere. It might be useful to explore this in studies of persons with focal slow activity by employing tests of perception for degraded speech, such as those described in this book, in order to tax the verbal processing function in such persons.

The most prominent of the EEG waves, the alpha rhythms, normally of a frequency of 8–13 Hz, generally decline slowly with aging, although almost one-quarter of *Ss* studied show an increase (Wang and Busse, 1969). The tentative explanation of the slowing of the alpha rhythm with age is vascular insufficiency. In fact, Marsh and Thompson (1977), after reviewing various suggested mechanisms underlying age-related changes in function, leaned toward hypotheses based upon changing flow of blood to the brain.

A reported observation that there are long-lasting "after effects" of cerebral activity in older persons, as seen in EEG studies (Timiras and Vernadakis, 1972), may explain in part the reports in this book of the reduced ability of middle-age and older listeners to understand speech in which the time factors have been disturbed.

AGING AND SENSORY PERCEPTION

In past books on experimental psychology, the topic of perception drew mainly on phenomena of vision, such as space perception and visual illusion. This has been broadened considerably, and now perception can be looked upon as a strong pattern-recognition activity of the sensory areas, singly or in combination. In a memorable short course on auditory perception, given at the 1965 annual meeting of the American Speech and Hearing Association, J. D. Harris used the sense of taste to illustrate this: the tongue has fibers for salt and fibers for sour, but we use a combination of fibers to arrive at the patterned sensation of acid. He observed that our perceptions are governed by our expectations, and that many of these in turn are *learned* classifications (i.e., categorizations), although some categorizations, such as figure-ground, are probably innate. Thus, he suggested, our primitive perceptions are elaborated with experience, as we build up categories such as the cue-search (confirmation-search, or "search and check")—a progressive testing that uses cues to check against a hypothesis until we confirm our views of the probabilistic nature of the real world. He pointed out that we may reject additional cues that could yield a true perception. That is, once a false confirmation has been achieved, we may reject additional cues. It is suggested repeatedly in this book that this tendency of persisting in an error perception is seen more in older than in younger subjects.

Corso (1971) reviewed published reports on changes with age in various human sensory functions. The following draws upon his review as well as upon other published material as noted.

Vision

There are structural changes with age in the lens size, thickness, and permeability for light. Thus a reduced amount of light enters the eye with age. Visual activity declines, particularly after the 50s, and accommodation of the muscle responsible for adjusting the focal length of the lens is reduced, resulting in presbyopia, a limiting of the depth of focus. In a section on visual perception, Miles (1942) reported detailed results, for closely contiguous age groupings, on the accuracy of recognizing visual patterns, e.g., letters, numbers, short sentences, groups of lines, and common expressions faultily written, all of which were presented in short exposures via a tachistoscope. He showed a rise in performance from childhood to young adulthood, and then a marked decline after the age of 55. Miles summarized his impression that "perception is not as prompt in the old as in the young, and its span is shorter." This insightful observation apparently explains the report, in Corso's (1971) review, that older persons showed less ability to extract information from complex visual stimuli; as Fozard et al. (1977) stated, "longer search times for a target imbedded in a complex static display would be expected for older persons." Even in simple recognition of one element in a static display, such as noting the position of a gap in a ring, older persons require more time than younger subjects. The disadvantage, for older Ss, becomes proportionately greater if the target to be identified is in motion.

The role of slower time integration in older Ss is cited also by Wallace (1956), who reported that when Ss were required to identify visual displays from sequential presentation of their parts, they could perform this task as well as younger Ss only when the displays were simple. As the displays became more complicated, requiring more integration over time, there was progressive age decrement in performance.

Another measure that may involve integration time is known as critical flicker fusion (CCF). An example of this is the maximum speed of flashes of light before the flashes appear to the observer to be a continuous light. Older Ss tend to report a continuous signal when there are fewer flashes per second, indicating that they are less efficient than younger Ss in discriminating the on-off pattern of more rapidly flickering signals (Woodruff, 1975).

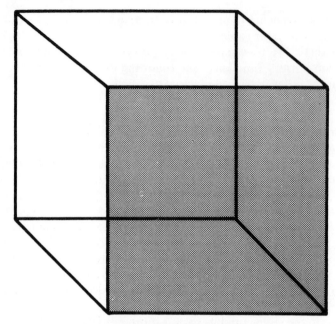

Figure 2.2.   Necker cube illusion.

Further evidence of age-related decrement in the time domain is the slowing of reactions, measured in reaction time (RT), to controlled stimuli. This is apparently a common aspect of aging, and according to Birren (1965) occurs in any person who survives beyond adulthood. Simply put, "Older people perform more slowly than young" (Woodruff, 1975).

Lansing, Schwartz, and Lindley (1959) and Surwillo (1961, 1963), after studying the relationship between RT and EEG alpha speed, concluded that frequency of the EEG is the CNS factor behind age-associated slowing in the lengthened time required for responses by older persons.

It is often stated that older persons tend to be rigid. Botwinick (1971) encapsulated this: "On more tests and with more tasks than not, the elderly make scores indicative of difficulty of overcoming ongoing patterns of behavior that are no longer adequate." Corso (1971) noted this for the field of visual perception, where it is seen that older persons tend to accept their first perception of a stimulus and resist changing that perception. (Repeated observation of this in audition is reported in a number of studies described in this book.) Examples of such relative inflexibility have been reported in studies of visual perception where aging Ss are less able to perceive the two separate figures (e.g., the faces of a young lady and an old woman) drawn ambiguously in a single illustration even after being shown one of the figures separately. Similarly, older Ss could not experience reversals of the Necker cube as younger ones could (Figure 2.2).

Aside from age-related changes in the eye's structure and their consequences for visual changes, therefore, alterations in visual perceptual tasks seem to center on a slowing of information processing together with the increasing perceptual inflexibility that tends to resist changes in image judgment.

Other Senses

The sense of touch declines with age, as the skin's elasticity is reduced and tactile and pain receptors and most of our taste buds are lost. (Fortunately, taste is partly a learned ability, so we can look forward to gourmet enjoyment even in general decline.) Loss of nasal sensory receptors results in deterioration of the sense of smell. Changes reported for other sensory modalities, such as gustation, olfaction, and tactile and pain sensitivity and tolerance limits, do not, however, seem to involve complex perceptual functions comparable to those of vision and audition.

In his summary, Corso (1971) noted that while there are age decrements in a number of sensory functions, occurring at various ages and proceeding at different rates, "visual and auditory impairments play a primary role in mediating the poorer performance often observed in old *Ss* on psychological tests."

In sensory perception, as in other areas, gerontological research at present appears to be concerned with *descriptions* of changes that accompany the aging process and studies of the *mechanisms* of the observed changes.

The emphasis in this book is largely on descriptive accounts of phenomena of aging perception of speech, with little attempt, at this stage, to develop prescriptive methodology for reducing their undesirable effects. Many of the findings herein, however, such as the effects of transmitting devices like the telephone and the hearing aid and the linguistic aspects that impair the understanding of speech by older listeners, strongly suggest environmental changes that can be beneficial.

Aging Memory

Understandably, auditory and visual stimuli dominate studies of memory, with an apparent emphasis on auditory stimuli, which can be presented so conveniently to subjects. A detailed report of important studies of aging and memory is found in Craik (1968).

It is evident that messages that are heard, in contrast to those that are read, are fleeting in each of their parts and therefore require the memory, or storage, of portions while additional parts continue to pass rapidly. It

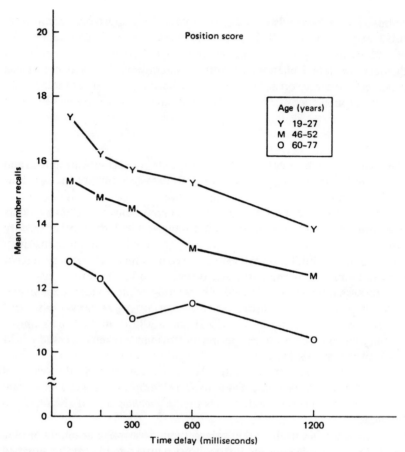

Figure 2.3.   The progressive decline, from young through middle-age and older adults, in the number of letters reported correctly from tachistoscopic arrays, as a function of time delay of a signal indicating what the subject must report. (From D. S. Woodruff and J. E. Birren (eds.), *Aging: Scientific Perspectives and Social Issues,* © 1975 by Litton Educational Publishing, Inc. Reprinted by permission of Van Nostrand Reinhold Co., New York.)

is only a possible auditory "echoing" and short-term memory that permit the listener to relate what he has just heard to what he is momentarily hearing. That is, although we can re-read a missed printed sentence or passage, we can re-hear only in our auditory memory, unless we ask the talker to repeat. It is notable, therefore, that older listeners seem to make this request often.

The progressive aging deterioration in storage capacity, from young through middle-age and older adulthood, so important to the understanding of a spoken message, can be demonstrated for vision through the use of the exposure-time control of the tachistoscope, as applied by Abel, cited in Walsh (1975), who converted Abel's (1972) tabular data (Figure 2.3).

As a background for discussions of aging speech perception it should be useful to relate memory to the various stages of input reception.

Craik (1977) reported that the terms *short-term memory (STM)* and *long-term memory (LTM)* are being replaced by *primary memory (PM)*, for items still in conscious awareness, and *secondary memory (SM)*, for long-term storage. Peterson (1966) suggested that the short-term memory stages result in neuronal activity, which fades out if not repeated, while the longer term memory results in the structural, neuronal changes that lead to storage and that therefore can be recalled.

Various studies have noted that the earliest stages of memory, during a perception, do not seem to suffer deterioration with aging. A frequently cited support for this observation is the consistent finding that auditory memory span (the number of words or digits that a person can repeat immediately after hearing them) remains unimpaired with age, unless the range generally recalled successfully even by young adults is exceeded. The amount of material included in the memory span seems to depend upon unit *meaning* rather than numbers of units alone. Thus, while single-letter messages are retained better than two- or three-letter messages, words in which the letters are familiarly related enjoy as good retention as single letters (Peterson, 1966). This is apparently due to the more efficient registering into the memory system of items that are reasonably put together in groups, a process referred to as *chunking*. Each of us apparently employs this system not only for remembering long telephone numbers but also for understanding poorly heard phrases or sentences. That is, the contextual probabilities, mainly caused by syntax and semantics, aid us by placing certain constraints on the material.

A reasonable question, then, is whether the linguistic and related constraints that facilitate the chunking of heard messages into the memory system decay with age.

In one approach to this, Craik (1968) employed word lists developed by Miller and Selfridge (1950), in which the word sequences to be recalled by *Ss* are graded, from being unrelated to each other through increasing degrees of relatedness until they finally form standard English text. After testing different age groups of adults, he found, as expected, that as the redundancy increased (that is, as the words became more related to each other as they approached standard English), both young and older *Ss* recalled more of the words in the lists, but that this improvement was less in the older listeners (see Figure 2.4). In other words, the contribution of contextual constraints to auditory material seems to weaken with aging.

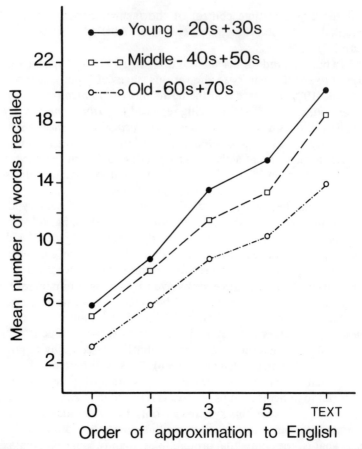

Figure 2.4.   Average number of words recalled by *Ss* of three age groups from 30-word lists of different approximations of relatedness, up to standard English text. (Data from Craik, 1968, Table III, p. 143.)

In comparing the short-term memory for vision with audition, Peterson (1966) reported that auditory forgetting is much quicker than visual forgetting, and Boyle et al. (1975) compared auditory memory for spoken word pairs with visual memory for designs and design pairs and found that auditory STM tested in this way showed *less* age decrement than visual STM.

Craik (1968) interpreted his experimental results as indicating that aging primarily affects the function of registering into and retrieving material from the long-term memory, but that aging has little effect on the recall of material from primary (or "echo box") storage.

If what is heard must be kept in storage during another activity, its retrieval is relatively impaired in older persons. Inglis and Caird (1963)

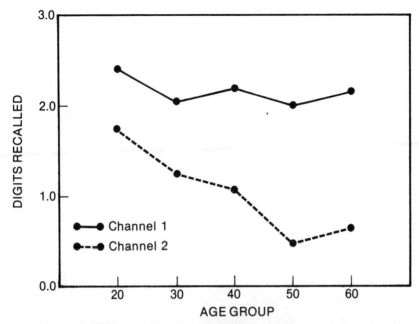

Figure 2.5.   Recall of first half-set (channel 1) of dichotic digits vs. second half-set (channel 2) as a function of age. (From J. E. Birren and K. W. Schaie (eds.), *Handbook of the Psychology of Aging,* p. 389, © 1977 by Litton Educational Publishing, Inc. Reprinted by permission of Van Nostrand Reinhold Co., New York.)

published an important report on their studies in which short sets of digits were presented dichotically, requiring one half-set to be held in storage by the subject while he reports the other half-set. They documented that there is no age-related decrement in the immediate recall of the first half-set, but the stored second half-set shows rapid decline with increasing age (Figure 2.5). Similarly, when the range of probable items to be recalled is large, as in the recall of word lists taken from large possible vocabularies, Craik (1968) found clear age-related deficits.

Chapter 8 presents similar findings in the decreased relative performance of older subjects as the number of alternative possibilities, on a test of hearing for words, is increased.

It is now believed that at least part of the memory problem is due to slowdown in input handling efficiency. This seems to be supported by our research results, particularly those reported on the influence of the temporal aspects of the speech signal on its perception (see Chapter 7).

CHAPTER 3

PRESBYCUSIS AND OTHER AGE-RELATED CHANGES IN THE PERIPHERAL MECHANISM OF AUDITION

CONTENTS

The perception of speech is a complex activity involving the peripheral organ of hearing, auditory neural pathways, auditory cortex areas, and related cortical areas for linguistic functions, such as memory and association. Integrity of the peripheral organ is manifested by an adequate sensitivity of threshold and appropriate analysis of incoming signals by frequency, intensity, and temporal patterns. That is, it must be able to respond to the various *levels* of speech and to translate the various *sounds* of speech into the neural equivalents of those acoustic aspects that will permit the brain to differentiate and recognize speech and voice *patterns*. Fortunately, there is so much redundancy in most of our utterances that even sizable errors in the way the units and clusters of speech and voice sounds are produced by a talker or heard by the listener may not defeat the recognition of a message. The peripheral organ (Figure 3.1) is nevertheless the port of entry to the auditory system, and errors suffered there can cause embarrassing misunderstandings.

The most common change in the function of the peripheral ear with aging is in the reduction of its sensitivity to certain speech sounds by the inner ear. This often results in the inability of an older listener to differentiate acoustically similar words, such as *fifty* vs. *sixty.*

COCHLEAR PRESBYCUSIS

One of the first people to test human hearing for various tone frequencies was Sir Francis Galton, a cousin of Charles Darwin. At the International Health Exhibition in London in 1884, he tested almost 10,000 males and

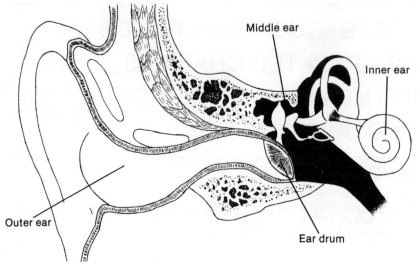

Figure 3.1.   The ear (schematic).

females, from ages 5 through 80, on a number of characteristics, among which was hearing. Since this preceded by many years the advent of the electronic audiometer, he fashioned a series of whistles that were tuned by varying their volume (Birren and Clayton, 1975). These "Galton whistles," as they became known to otologists, established that older listeners could no longer hear the higher tones.

Clinical evidence of such change has been the subject of publications since Zwaardemaker (1899) first described his findings of increasing loss of hearing for higher frequencies beginning about the second or third decade of life. Unfortunately, few of the curves published by various investigators agree on the rate of decline of hearing for the various audiometric frequencies, and except for the limited information available on clinical populations, the effects on the understanding of speech accompanying the decreasing sensitivity for audiometric tones have been relatively neglected. This is particularly understandable when the studies are carried out by researchers who test populations in remote areas of the world where the language is unfamiliar to them.

There are four main reasons why the published curves of presbycusis differ so much from each other.

1.   The calibration of the audiometers in the past was based upon standards determined in the researcher's country and were verified only by test equipment available to him. More recently there has been international agreement on calibration standards for pure tone audiometers, but standardization of the test equipment is still a problem.

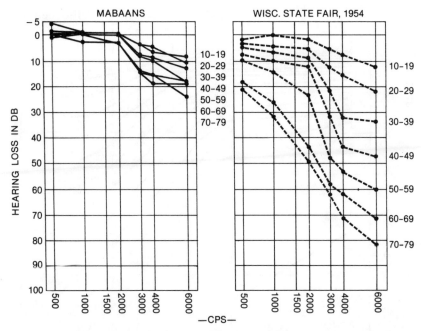

Figure 3.2. Aging audiograms for men. (From S. Rosen et al., *Annals of Otology, Rhinology and Laryngology 71*, p. 731, 1962, with permission.)

Particularly troubling is the tendency of some audiometers to attenuate nonlinearly at the lower hearing levels where the best hearers of a test population respond. The references for "normal" thresholds in such populations, therefore, may be contaminated by attenuation errors in the audiometers employed.

2. The ambient noise of the test area may influence the resultant thresholds, particularly for the frequencies lower than 1000 Hz. The use of special sound-isolated test booths and good earphone seals reduces this variable.

3. The technique of the testers can influence the data collected. Unfortunately, there has been little discussion or agreement on ways of standardizing techniques for threshold finding in audiometry for the study of presbycusis in general (nonclinic) populations.

4. The largest single variable in studies of presbycusis lies in the population samples tested. This is clearly seen in the sets of curves collected from studies conducted in diverse areas of the world.

Figure 3.2 shows the marked difference in median audiometric data for successive age decades of men, out of a total test population of 2585 residents of Wisconsin (Glorig et al., 1957) and for 541 primitive people, the

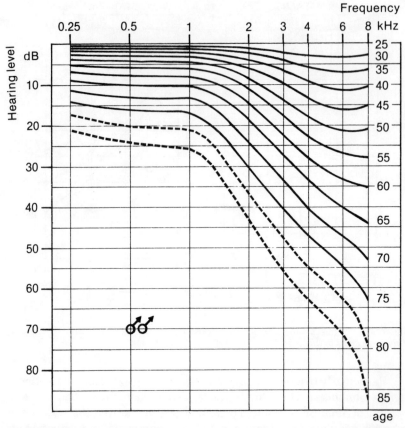

Figure 3.3. Aging audiograms for men. (From A. Spoor, *International Audiology 6,* pp. 47–58, 1967, with permission.)

Mabaans, in the middle of the Sudan (Rosen et al., 1962). Both studies were conducted very carefully with attention to audiometer calibration and in environments of low ambient noise. Except for one threshold at 6000 Hz, all data points for the Mabaan population up to age 79 fall close to the audiometric levels of the 20- to 29-year old subjects in the Wisconsin study; in contrast, significant age-related changes begin to occur *after* age 29 in the Wisconsin study group. (For numerical values for Glorig et al.'s study, see their p. 23.)

Further variations in curves purporting to represent presbycusis are shown in Figures 3.3 and 3.4. Figure 3.3 shows curves published by Spoor (1967) based upon the consolidated data of eight different publications on presbycusis from the United States, Denmark, Germany, and England. Figure 3.4 shows curves based upon almost 900 subjects studied by Jatho

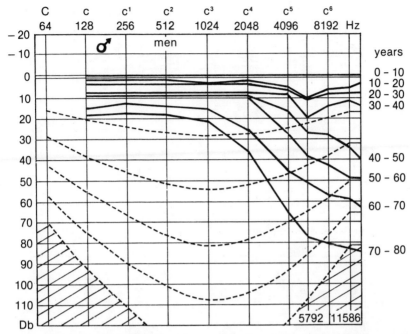

Figure 3.4.   Aging audiograms for men. (From K. Jatho, *International Audiology* 8(2-3), pp. 231-239, 1969, with permission.)

(1969), apparently in West Germany. The lack of agreement of the curves of age-related loss of hearing by audiometry is apparent.

Even differences in the age-related patterns of the sexes are influenced by the population sampled. Figure 3.5 indicates that the sex differences shown in studies conducted in the U.S. by various investigators (Bunch, 1929; Steinberg, Montgomery, and Gardner, 1940; Webster, Himes, and Lichtenstein, 1950) are clearly not the same as those found among the Mabaans (Rosen et al., 1962).

Although some published statements report that populations in some remote areas have hearing that at all ages is superior to that found in American and other Western studies (Rosen and Olin, 1965; Stevens and Warshofsky, 1965), the evidence is otherwise. For example, studies of the Kalahari Bushmen in South Africa (van der Sandt, Glorig, and Dickson, 1969) and of various tribes in Mauretania and Senegal (Reynaud, Camara, and Basteria, 1969) showed inferior hearing for those populations, apparently associated with middle ear disease; the Mabaans showed hearing that is not superior to that of low noise-exposed Americans until the age decade 60-69, where their thresholds for frequencies above 1000 Hz are better (Bergman, 1966). On the other hand, there have been

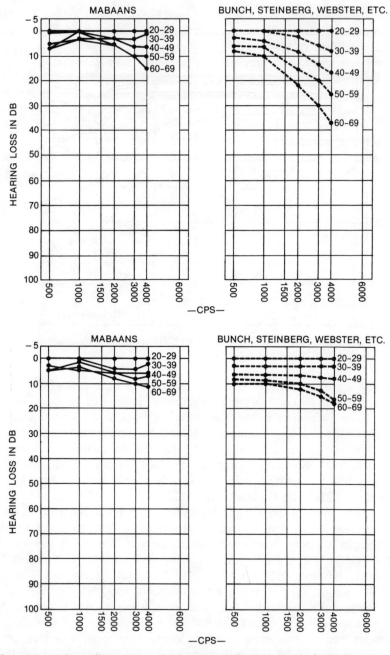

Figure 3.5.   Aging audiograms, men (top) vs. women (bottom). Results for the 20- to 2-year group are plotted as zero reference for all groups. (From S. Rosen et al., *Annals of Otology, Rhinology and Laryngology 71*, pp. 733–734, 1962, with permission.)

repeated reports (e.g., Bunch and Raiford, 1931; Post, 1964) of findings in American studies of the superiority, with aging, of hearing for the higher audiometric tones by black, compared to nonblack subjects. Post's report was based upon previously unpublished data from the New York World's Fair, supplied to him by Montgomery, one of the authors of the original Steinberg et al. (1940) report. More recently, Karsai, Bergman, and Choo (1972) tested 836 longshoremen in New York City and grouped their data according to the ethnic backgrounds represented and by the subjects' years of employment in that work—effectively, therefore, by similar ages. Their results clearly show better hearing for the frequencies 4000 and 8000 Hz by the black subjects throughout most of the ages implied by years of employment (Figure 3.6). In the same year, Eisdorfer and Wilkie (1972), in a study of limited samples, also reported that American Negroes in their 60s and 70s had significantly better hearing at all audiometric frequencies, even when followed up 7 years later.

A contradictory report is contained in the results obtained in the 1960–1962 National Health Survey (National Center for Health Statistics, 1967), in which no racial differences were found for the higher audiometric frequencies in older persons.

SPEECH PERCEPTION AND THE PATHOLOGY OF PRESBYCUSIS

Since the understanding of speech requires, as a beginning, that the peripheral hearing mechanism receive and transmit the signal with appropriate fidelity, it is useful to note any age-related changes in its function. There is little evidence that the outer and middle ear contribute significantly to age-related attenuation or distortion of incoming signals. The exquisite simplicity of the action of the middle ear, in fact, led the eminent ear physiologist Merle Lawrence to write (1958): "It is really quite astounding to find how truly linear the middle ear is in response to sounds of increasing intensity." He and many others have concluded, therefore, that it is the inner ear that is the seat of peripheral hearing changes with age.

Schuknecht (1955, 1964) and his colleagues (Gacek and Schuknecht, 1969; Schuknecht and Igarashi, 1964) have at various times published their observations on the pathological processes in the peripheral auditory mechanism that accompany the age-related audiograms in presbycusis. They also suggested the speech discrimination performance that would accompany each pathology. The changes seen by them are grouped into four categories, beginning with a commonly seen type that causes the high tone loss audiogram. They call this sensory presbycusis, to indicate atrophic changes in the basal turn of the cochlea, with a loss of hair cells and supporting structures. Figure 3.7 shows graphically the loss of many

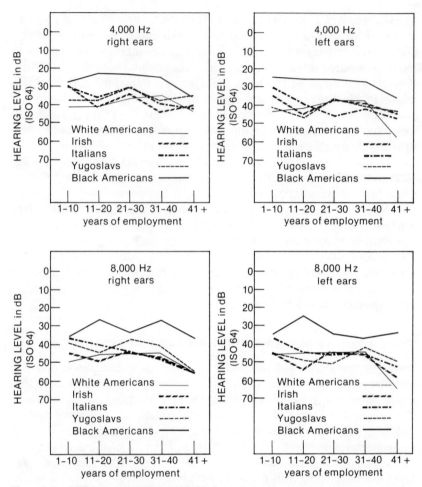

Figure 3.6.   Differences at 4000 and 8000 Hz for each decade of employment. The superiority of the black longshoremen is clear except for those employed over 41 years, the data for whom are based upon similar numbers of subjects. (From L. K. Karsai et al., *Archives of Otolaryngology 96*, p. 502, 1972, with permission. Copyright © 1972, American Medical Association.)

hair cells and the abnormality of others, particularly, in the basal turn of the cochlea up to about 12 mm from the base. The accompanying audiogram shows a sharp drop in sensitivity for tones above 2000 Hz, apparently closely correlated to the loss of hair cells. The "speech frequencies" (usually meaning from 500 to 2000 Hz) are reported not to be involved, implying little effect on the discrimination of speech, but such high tone losses in older persons will generally create considerable difficulties in understanding speech heard under other than optimal conditions. Although

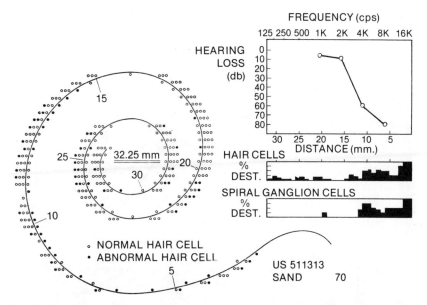

Figure 3.7. Graphic illustration of presbycusis pathology. The barograms indicate the percentages of hair and ganglion cells destroyed in the cochlea as a function of distance from the end of the basilar membrane. (From R. R. Gacek and H. F. Schuknecht, *International Audiology* 8(2–3), pp. 199–207, 1969, with permission.)

in persons with such audiograms the discrimination of speech heard in a one-to-one listener-talker situation does not usually suggest serious auditory problems, this is a misleading observation if it is interpreted to mean the absence of a disturbance in the person's daily life activities.

Sharp high tone losses on audiograms may be accompanied by a variety of degrees of disturbance of speech perception, often depending upon the frequency at which the audiogram suddenly descends. Figure 3.8 shows discrimination scores obtained on the usual clinic tests of performance on phonetically balanced (PB) word lists from patients with the audiograms shown. It should be noted, however, that there is considerable variation in speech discrimination performance within similar audiograms in clinic patients seen in audiology centers.

The second type of presbycusis pathology identified by the Schuknecht group is called neural loss, indicating loss of spiral ganglion cells and nerve fibers. Such pathology characteristically yields a relatively flat audiogram of moderate degree, and is accompanied by a marked difficulty in the discrimination of various speech sounds, beyond what would be expected with such a relatively uniform loss of hearing for pure tones.

The third type of pathology, according to these authors, disturbs the metabolic activity of the cochlea, apparently because of atrophy of the

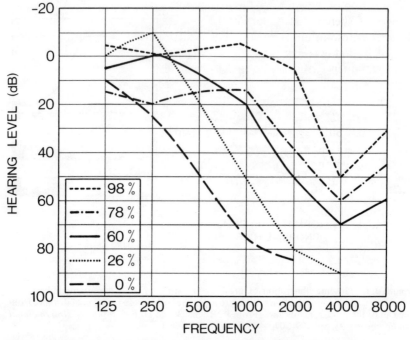

Figure 3.8.   Word discrimination scores associated with various audiograms.

stria vascularis. Since this is a disorder of the entire cochlea, the audiometric hearing loss tends to be flat, as in the neural loss cases, but in contrast to those losses, the so-called metabolic presbycusis pathology does
not interfere with the discrimination of speech, which is often normal or
near normal.

Finally, according to the Schuknecht group, presbycusis may result
from mechanical changes of the organ of Corti or of the stria vascularis,
which probably adversely affects the motion of such parts. The audiogram associated with such changes shows gradual loss of hearing toward
the higher frequencies, and results in increasing loss of speech discrimination as the audiometric loss grows progressively steeper over the years.

OTHER MALFUNCTIONS
OF THE PERIPHERAL HEARING MECHANISM

As we shall see in later chapters, any distortions of the speech signal make
it more difficult for an older listener to understand than for a younger
listener. It is important to note, therefore, that the loss of sensitivity for
low intensity sounds is not the only indication of undesirable change in

the function of the cochlea. There is abundant clinical and published evidence that there is disturbance of the loudness growth function and of the frequency resolution in ears that have suffered sensory changes. It is possible also that even the time domain may be disturbed, as in distinguishing the sequence of phonemes, but there are few data to support this at present.

We have suspected for some time that even before there is audiometric evidence of presbycusis there may be subtle changes in the function of the cochlea. Such changes, if they exist, could be related to the experimental findings that the perception of speech under certain conditions is significantly poorer in listeners in their 40s than in 20- to 30-year-olds, as reported in this book. Accordingly, we conducted a preliminary study using the aural overload test on middle-age and young adults. This procedure, described by Lawrence (1958) and his colleagues (Lawrence and Blanchard, 1954; Lawrence and Yantis, 1956) determines the range of intensities that can be processed by the inner ear before it begins to distort the incoming signal. This distortion, in which the ear produces extra sounds (harmonics) not found in the signal itself, occurs well above the threshold (about 50 dB or more) of the normal ear, for signal frequencies of 500 to 2000 Hz. There is evidence that in pathological inner ears the level at which such distortion begins is somewhat closer to the threshold. That is, the range of linearity of the ear's function may be reduced to only about 10 dB. Lawrence supplies compelling arguments, from analogy to the clear electrophysiological evidence on animal ears, that this test does reveal distortion in the inner ear. Unfortunately, the human version, in which the listener must detect and report the appearance of a beating tone, is very difficult, which accounts for the waning of interest in its use clinically after an initial enthusiastic reaction by audiologists and otologists.

Our study employed a simplified testing technique recently proposed by Hume (1978). Sensation levels of the beginning of the aural harmonics in 38 ears of Ss ages 20–29 vs. 40 ears of Ss ages 40–49 years were explored. All Ss, both young and middle-age, were required to have hearing within normal limits, with no audiometrically suggestive signs of presbycusis. Only 1000 Hz was tested in this study, because although it was recognized that age-related dysfunction would be most apt to occur in the vicinity of 4000 Hz, it was technically more convenient to study the generation of harmonics of 1000 Hz.

The results are seen in Figure 3.9, which also includes the original findings by Lawrence (1958), using a somewhat different technique. Our average sensation level for the normal ears was similar to Lawrence's, but our standard deviation was smaller, possibly indicating greater homoge-

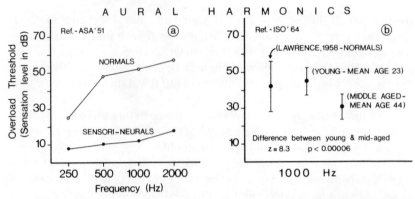

Figure 3.9.   a, Aural harmonics sensation levels at various probe tones, as reported by Lawrence (1958). b, Our results for a 1000-Hz probe tone, young vs. middle-age adults who have normal audiograms. (Lawrence's datum, corrected for ISO '64, for that probe tone is included for reference.)

neity of our population. The difference between the range of linearity in the young adults and in the "normal" ears of the middle-age Ss is clear and highly significant ($p < 0.0001$). The suspicion that there may be early distortions in the inner ear before the emergence of clinical (i.e., audiometric) signs of presbycusis seems to be supported in this study.

Another test that might be applied to otherwise normal ears of middle-age and young adults explores the listener's ability to detect small increments or decrements of intensity and frequency. If there are changes in the inner ear, an abnormally *increased* ability to detect small intensity changes (the "recruitment" phenomenon) and *decreased* detection of small changes in the signal frequency would be expected to result. Konig (1957) published his findings on the changes in the difference limen (differential sensitivity) for frequency (DLF) as a function of increasing age (Figure 3.10). It appears that at least for the higher audiometric frequencies the DLF of older persons is larger than normal for young listeners.

Unfortunately, while there are many published articles relating such tests to pathological ears, they have not yet been applied to broadly sampled nonclinic older populations who have minimal or absent clinical signs.

While the understanding of speech depends only in part on the accuracy of the neural code provided to the brain by the peripheral coding mechanism, it has become clear that for the aging brain the reduced amount of accurate information reaching it causes significantly more problems than in younger persons, such as those who serve as subjects in most of the published psychoacoustic studies of the phenomena of speech perception.

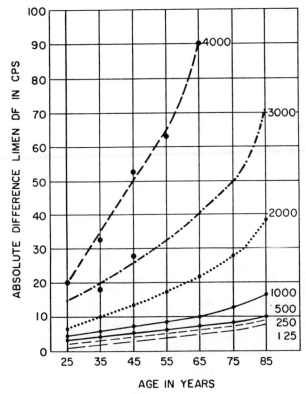

Figure 3.10.   Difference limens for frequency as a function of age. (From E. Konig, 1957, *Acta Oto-laryngologica 48*, pp. 475–489. Reprinted by permission of S. Karger AG, Basel.)

SUMMARY

It is well established that with advancing age many persons show audiometric changes of the various types described in this chapter. Such change in sensitivity for low intensity sounds generally affects the understanding of speech by eliminating certain speech sounds from audibility. Furthermore, because of alterations in the complex aspects of the inner ear's function as a transducer of mechanical to neuronal energy, it may be that even those sounds that are still audible to the listener are distorted because of altered intensity and frequency resolution in the peripheral hearing system. It is reasonable to conclude, therefore, that the neural code for speech that must be transmitted from the peripheral organ and its associated structures to the brain may be adversely affected even in the earliest stages of aging, requiring a more difficult decoding task of the central system. This might explain in part the decrease in the perception of some forms of degraded speech, beginning in early middle age.

CHAPTER 4

NEURAL BASES OF
AGING SPEECH PERCEPTION

CONTENTS

The brain is extremely complex in its network of interrelated parts. For example, Rosenblith (1969) stated that it has 10 billion neurons and possibly 100 times as many satellite cells, and even more complex superimposing of other neurons on *these* neurons, monitoring their synapsing. This bountiful elaborateness supports the notion of its function as an *integrating* system rather than of a generating, transmitting, and receiving system for individual neural events, such as those related to the elements of speech.

We would very much like to know the location and function of the neural mechanisms most directly responsible for the various stages in the processing of a spoken message, from the reception and differentiation of phonetic and related features through the syntactic and semantic organization associated with understanding. Therefore, it is tempting to develop a model that would illuminate the hierarchical dichotomies of physiology and behavior that are involved. Such knowledge might guide us in our investigations of the neural bases of aging speech perception. Alas, we are simply not ready for this; as Stevens and House (1972) put it, "Since we are still far from an understanding of the neurophysiological processes involved, any model that can be proposed must be a functional model and one can only *speculate* on the relation between the components of the functional model and the neural events at the periphery of the auditory system and in the central nervous system."

However, there are bits and pieces of evidence that, while falling short of a convincing model, suggest possible relationships to be pursued further.

THE BRAIN AND HIGHER MENTAL FUNCTIONS

The understanding of speech is certainly one of the more complex functions that the brain must perform. Attempts to understand the relationship between age-associated changes in its anatomy and physiology and the clear deterioration in the understanding of speech heard under difficult listening conditions, as reported in this book, must address themselves to the rich body of theory and knowledge developed at least since the times of Broca and Wernicke.

As in other study areas of human behavior, there have been contending schools of thought on the relative importance, to the higher cerebral function, of localized areas vs. complex integrative activity. Thus, even as Broca showed that motor speech is affected by lesions of specified parts of the lower frontal convolution of the left cortical hemisphere, his contemporary, Hughlings Jackson, argued that higher mental functions are related to the brain as a whole, attributing less influence to the function of localized parts (Luria, 1964/1965). As viewed retrospectively by Luria, this was the historical beginning of the two schools of localizationists and antilocalizationists.

A helpful theoretical model that attempts to integrate the contributions of localized brain areas and generalized brain function, in higher mental processes, is Luria's formulation of "complex functional systems" (Luria, 1973), in which he sees various zones of the brain working together jointly as a product of the individual's cumulative history in a social environment. He recognizes the importance of local function by stressing that the destruction of "any link" of the complex functional system may impair higher mental functions: "When one or another link has been lost, the whole functional system will be disturbed in a particular way" (Luria, 1964/1965).

These attempts by psychological investigators to explain the relationship between disturbance in mental function and localized brain damage have provided a useful background for current research on a variety of central functions, such as perception, memory, and association, so essential to language behavior.

THE AGING BRAIN

Age-related changes in the auditory nervous system are not independent of general changes in the central nervous system. The brain apparently shrinks, with aging, although estimates on the amount vary. For example, Shock (1962) reported the loss of 44% of brain weight from ages 30 to 75, with a decrease in the flow of blood to the brain of 20%. Von Braunmühl (1957) reported a 16.4% drop from ages 20 to 80 (also cited in Konigsmark, 1969b), and Smith and Sethi (1975) suggested a 160- to 200-g loss (about 11.5% to 14%). This loss of weight alone does not indicate the full extent of the loss of brain cells, since such cells are replaced by connective tissue and remaining neurons are often atrophic. It is important to note that loss or alteration of neurons in the central nervous system is apparently selective, with the most reported changes occurring in those areas believed to be most involved with the understanding of speech. Thus, Brody (1955) found the greatest loss of neuronal population, in the human brain, to be in the superior temporal gyrus, with the inferior temporal gyrus being intermediate. Samorajski (1976) reported that the narrowed gyri and deepened and widened sulci seen in the shrunken older brain are "usually prominent in the superior frontal and temporal lobes." As in all attempts to relate reported loss of neurons to changes in function, however, such reports are based upon morphological examinations that involve problems of sampling and specimen preparation.

Although the posterior part of the temporal area is so important to audition that bilateral lesions in that part of the Sylvian fissure will produce cortical deafness (Roberts, 1966), "lesions in the inferior medial temporal region induce disturbances in immediate memory." Chapter 9 reports our first findings on the role of memory in speech perception with aging.

Another approach that attempts to observe function employs electroencephalographic (EEG) studies. Smith and Sethi (1975) reported that in over 33% of elderly persons there is a slowing in brain-wave electrical activity, particularly over the anterior areas, and *sometimes more on the left side*. This may be significant, because as Roberts (1966) pointed out, serious disturbances in speech occur with lesions of the posterior temporal, inferior parietal, and anterior occipital regions, but "the more anterior the lesion the more auditory aspects of speech are involved."

The time-processing difficulties in aging speech perception, reported here, may be related to a slowing of the basic alpha frequency seen in EEG recordings of older persons (Figure 4.1). The possible import of this was expressed by Smith and Sethi (1975): "Prominent among the changes is slowness of performance caused not so much by reduced sensory activity . . . as by a delay in central reaction time, with the patient requiring longer periods for recognition and response to stimuli."

In addition to the search for cortical changes that may affect the perception of speech, the possible role of lower areas of the brain and its stem should not be overlooked. For example, in a thought-provoking article on the case of a young, "congenitally aphasic" boy, Landau, Goldstein, and Kleffner (1960) reported their findings on his difficulties in understanding speech at the age of 6, his improvement through intensive training during the next 4 years, and the histological study performed after he died suddenly, apparently after cardiac complications, at the age of 10. Summarizing the pathological findings, they reported "severe damage to the

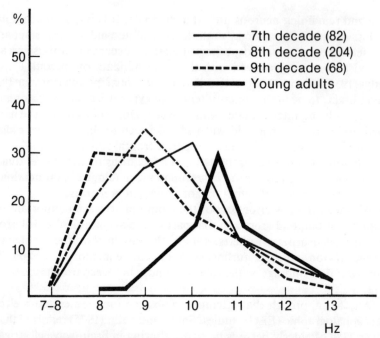

Figure 4.1.   Distribution curves of frequencies of the dominant alpha waves in various age decades of normal adults. The numbers in parentheses indicate the number of subjects in each group. (From E. Otomo, *Electroencephalography and Clinical Neuro-physiology*, Vol. 21, pp. 489–491, 1966, Elsevier/North-Holland Biomedical Press, Amsterdam, with permission.)

primary auditory projection pathways bilaterally, with corresponding retrograde degeneration of the medial geniculate nuclei.''

Despite the availability at present of considerable knowledge of the anatomy of both the peripheral and central auditory systems, it is clear that we are still without sufficient information about their separate and interrelated functions in the understanding of speech to relate even the meager evidence of brain changes to behavioral findings.

AGE-RELATED CHANGES IN
THE AUDITORY SYSTEM AND ITS FUNCTION

The best reported changes in the listening mechanism are those of the peripheral auditory system, discussed in the previous chapter on presbycusis. The interference with the discrimination of the phonemes of speech when the peripheral ear mechanism deteriorates is well documented in the daily experience of the audiologist. It has been suggested (Abbs and Sussman, 1971) that there are neurons of the central auditory system that detect and process the acoustic characteristics of individual phonetic features of speech. This theory relies upon the additional hypothesis that there is peripheral "sharpening" of variations (i.e., deviations) of incoming phonemes to result in their accurate perception. Under this formulation, if the auditory changes, with aging, were only peripheral, as suggested by the threshold shifts revealed by pure tone audiometry, it would seem that speech that is distorted, either before entering the ear or in the ear's peripheral mechanism, should be heard about as well by older as by younger listeners with similar hearing. The evidence is otherwise. This does not rule out the possibility that there may, in fact, be neuronal cells in the brainstem or in the cortex that are specific "feature detectors" for speech, as argued by Abbs and Sussman, and that these deteriorate with age, either specifically or as part of general central changes.

Luria (1964/1965), inferring from performance on writing from oral dictation, stated that "destruction of the left temporal lobe (especially its upper posterior sections) leads to a disturbance of phonemic hearing." Similarly, the "phonemic regression" concept of Gaeth (1948), which suggests that the discrimination of the phonemes of speech is significantly worse in older persons than their peripheral hearing loss (presbycusis) would explain, may be fitted into such a neurological framework.

The functional change in a process as complex as the understanding of a spoken message would seem to be in overall integration at the highest level, based only in part on the nature of the neurally coded information transmitted from the ear via its associated central auditory nervous system. In addition, the usual speech message, with its setting and partially anticipated content, contains an overabundance of duplicated clues. It is this very fortuitous double elaboration, in the external message itself and in the internal processing system, that ordinarily protects against serious disruption of the perceptual process for understanding speech, even when the message is badly distorted before it reaches the listener or by mild disturbance of parts of the listener's auditory system, as in presbycusic changes in his peripheral ear mechanism or a reduction of function in the brain stem and midbrain.

The role of each part of the central auditory nervous system is still unclear, but it should be useful to summarize briefly the currently recognized structure of this mechanism and to consider published accounts of their apparent changes with age (see Figure 4.2).

It has long been known that the temporal lobe is the main cortical center for audition, with the superior temporal gyrus (Brodmann's areas 41, 42, and 22) containing the primary and secondary areas (see Figure 4.3). Penfield and Roberts (1959) emphasized that much of each temporal lobe includes the interpretive cortex.

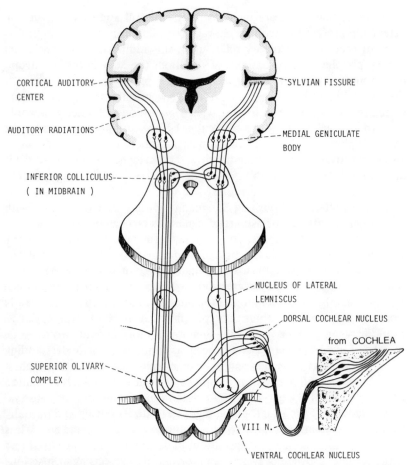

Figure 4.2.   The central auditory pathways. Fibers emerging from the internal auditory canal of the cochlea make up nerve VIII, which synapses in the dorsal and ventral cochlear nuclei, in the brain stem. The unilaterality of fibers from each ear then gives way to a large crossing over through the trapezoid body in the pons, where many of them enter the superior olivary nucleus complex on the other side. Here they turn and proceed up through the central acoustic pathway of the lateral lemniscus to the inferior colliculus at the head of the mid-brain. While a few fibers cross over the commissure of the colliculi to the other side, the main fibers move on to the medial geniculate body, which is a relay station in the diencephalon connecting the midbrain with the cerebral cortex. The radiations then end in Heschel's gyrus, where the auditory center is found in the fissure of Sylvius. Thus most of the fibers from each ear end up in the opposite cerebral hemisphere.

The importance of the most posterior association areas of the left temporal lobe and their connections to the primary auditory centers located more anteriorly in and around the Sylvian fissure should not be overlooked. Luria (1964/1965), relying on the apparent involvement of

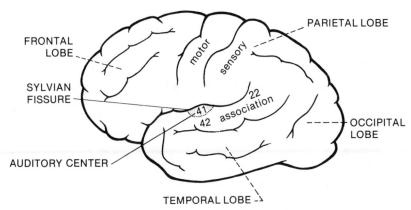

FRONTAL
LOBE

SYLVIAN
FISSURE

AUDITORY CENTER

PARIETAL LOBE

motor   sensory

22
41   association
42   association

OCCIPITAL
LOBE

TEMPORAL LOBE

Figure 4.3.   Left hemisphere of the brain showing the location of the primary auditory center (buried in the Sylvian fissure) and the auditory association area, in the temporal lobe.

the cortical areas for speech articulation in the understanding of oral dictation, emphasized the major role of the postcentral section of the left hemisphere in the kinesthetic analysis of incoming speech.

There are conflicting reports concerning central changes in the auditory system. Whereas Konigsmark (1969a) and Konigsmark and Murphy (1972) reported no age-related loss of neurons in the ventral cochlear nucleus, Kirikae, Sato, and Shitara (1964) noted that in senile patients there is degeneration at that level, as well as at the superior olive, the inferior colliculus, and the medial geniculate body, and Hansen and Reske-Nielsen (1965) also reported atrophy in various parts of the central auditory pathways and nuclei and in the cortex.

Once again the paucity of factual knowledge about the age-associated alterations of the central auditory system precludes a definitive discussion.

LANGUAGE FUNCTIONS AND THE BRAIN

Interest in the relationship between language functions (of which the perception of speech is one of the most important) and the anatomy, physiology, and pathology of the brain has grown steadily since the 19th century, when Broca demonstrated in 1961 that speech ability is affected by lesions of that part of the lower frontal area of the left hemisphere, which is now known by his name. Wernicke, 12 years later, attributed central deficits in the understanding of speech to impairment of the posterior third of the upper temporal convolution of the left hemisphere (Luria, 1964/1965). Subsequently, a steady succession of perceptive investigators of the brain and its function has led to the development of specialty areas, such as *neuropsychology* (a term proposed by Luria and his collaborators) and *neurolinguistics,* and to journals specifically linking the study of brain and language.

A major focus of published studies on the brain-language relationship is the interest in aphasia, and in lieu of sufficient literature on language function and aging, we must still attempt to draw some of our insights for aging studies from findings in brain lesions.

Among the more remarkable direct observations of the relationship between the function of specific areas of the brain and language and memory functions in nonaphasic patients, however, are those reported by Penfield and his associates at the Montreal Neurological Institute (Penfield and Roberts, 1959). As a treatment of focal epilepsy, Penfield's group removed pathological portions of the brain. By applying electrical stimulation to selected areas of the cortex during surgery performed under local anesthesia, they produced remarkable behavioral symptoms. For example, they were able to interfere with the ideational aspects of speech so that aphasia-like loss of the ability to name common objects occurred. When the stimulating electrode was removed, the patient could immediately supply the correct object names once again. By this method Penfield mapped the main cortical areas involved in the ideational processes of speech (as contrasted with the areas that are known to control the muscles and related activities used in its production). He showed that these cortical speech areas apparently perform similar functions, since electrical stimulation of each of them produced similar behavioral responses. The most critical area for the maintenance of speech appears to be in the posterior temporal lobe and its nearby regions.

An important additional observation by Penfield was that surgical removal of the cortical areas surrounding each of the speech areas did not result in aphasia symptoms. Because of the similarity of the behavioral effects of stimulating the various speech areas, it was suggested that they must be connected in some way. Since the areas between them do not seem to contribute to disturbance of speech when they are destroyed, it was suggested that connections between the speech areas is through the brain stem rather than the cortex. The existence of dense fiber tracts between the speech areas and the thalamus may be evidence of this.

HEMISPHERIC DOMINANCE IN SPEECH PERCEPTION

The major evidence today, as in the early work of Broca, places the dominant role for speech perception in the left hemisphere in most persons.

A rich source of information on the location of language function in the brain is the steadily accumulating literature on dichotic listening.

Dichotic listening is primarily a research procedure in which different messages, either verbal or nonverbal (e.g., musical passages) are presented simultaneously to the two ears, yielding responses that indicate which ear and cortical hemisphere combination seem to be dominant in this competing auditory perceptual task. For example, if one word is presented to the right ear simultaneously with another word to the left ear, a response containing only the right ear's word or both words in the order of right ear first and left ear second is interpreted to indicate right-ear dominance for that pair of stimuli. Since the neural auditory system more strongly connects each ear with its contralateral cortical hemisphere, the right ear superiority indicates left hemisphere dominance. There is now a very large body of literature based upon this technique that consistently locates the processing of language in the left hemisphere in most persons, whereas nonlinguistic, spatial, or cognitive processing functions occur dominantly in the right hemisphere. The dichotic listening technique has been employed to explore not only changes in auditory perceptual dominance, as a function of aging, but also aspects of short-term memory vs. aging (Inglis and Caird, 1963; Inglis and Tansey, 1967).

Much of the existing literature on the lateralization of language in the brain deals with early childhood, adolescence, and early maturity (college age). Johnson et al. (1979), in a study of hemisphere efficiency in the middle and later years, agreed that "there is a paucity of data dealing with the lateralization of hemispheric functioning of neurologically intact persons beyond early maturity," as our experience has shown. They attempted to add to our information with a report of two studies, using the dichotic listening approach, first testing dichotic memory for dual sets (one set to each ear) of two, three, and four digits. They included subjects from ages 50 to 79, divided into three groups of youngest, middle, and oldest. Their results substantiated the decline, with age, for material presented to the left ear (right cerebral hemisphere), whereas material to the right ear (left hemisphere) showed no discernible decrement. They suggested that there may be "a greater decline in persons' performance on the non-dominant than on the dominant hemisphere no matter what task is involved." Since this experiment tested only verbal memory, however—a primary left hemisphere ability—they proceeded with a second study that tested changes in performance on a musical note recognition task to determine whether there is decline in right hemisphere ability with age for functions that are primarily related to that side. The result revealed decline in *both* hemispheres, with age. They concluded, therefore, that: 1) on tasks that are left hemisphere dependent, the decline appears to take place only in the non-dominant hemisphere, and 2) those abilities, such as spatiality, that depend more on the right hemisphere may show a real decline, with age, for both dominant and nondominant hemispheres. An important inference from their studies is that the abilities that depend more on the left than the right hemisphere remain relatively intact with age, because the function of the dominant side does not decline.

An interesting study carried out on infants, children, and young adults (mean age of the latter was 26) by Molfese, Freeman, and Palermo (1975), in which they recorded auditory-evoked responses (AERs) from the temporal regions of both cerebral hemispheres in response to speech and nonspeech acoustic stimuli, yielded larger amplitude AERs from the left hemisphere in all groups when the stimulus was speech, and the reverse for the nonspeech stimuli. The amount of lateralization dominance decreased, however, with increasing subject age.

There remains little doubt about the left hemisphere's dominance for the perception of speech in most listeners, but the apparent further weakening of the nondominant hemisphere as a function of age needs additional substantiation.

SUMMARY

Luria (1964/1965) neatly pointed out that "demonstrated disturbances of specific functions can only provide a certain *probability* of corresponding local (neural) damage, but not complete assurance, which can only be obtained in the presence of a whole syndrome of symptoms." In a similar vein, gerontologists note that while there are age-related decrements in each of the body's organ systems that are involved in a particular activity, they are less than the decrement in total performance (Shock, 1977).

Despite the lack of evidence relating specific or generalized brain changes to the relative difficulty of middle-age and older listeners in the understanding of speech heard under less than optimal conditions, most findings clearly implicate the central nervous system. It remains for future research to delineate the intricacies and specifics of the neural mechanisms that are responsible for both normal and altered function in this complex activity.

CHAPTER 5

ORGANIZING STUDIES
OF AGING SPEECH PERCEPTION

CONTENTS

It is generally apparent that the study of age-related changes in the understanding of speech requires attention to a number of variables considerably more extensive than those represented in standard tests of hearing. The most general application of the latter has been in audiology clinics, where a limited number of tests are depended upon for the diagnosis of auditory pathology and for the testing of hearing with hearing aids. Surveys of population trends, on the other hand, as for the study of aging, have been concerned largely with a single measure: the loss of hearing sensitivity for audiometric test tones.

Those beginning the investigation of age-related changes in the understanding of spoken communication are immediately confronted by a host of new procedural problems to be solved. Not the least of these is the determination of how to draw population samples that will represent the broadest examples of the aging population. We must, of course, have first decided on whether we are interested in the entire life-span or only in the elderly and, if in the latter, define what *elderly* means. Since it is known that aging is often accompanied by basic changes in the hearing function, such as these represented by the term *presbycusis,* we must decide what standard of hearing to apply to subjects in each age group that we wish to include in our studies.

The next major question to resolve is what kind of test materials will appropriately illuminate the daily function of the population samples of our study. Should the tests consist of monosyllabic words that can be expected to expose phoneme reception errors, or more typically redundant materials, such as sentences?

Typical life situation listening includes hearing speech under a variety of conditions, such as quiet, noisy, reverberant, or transmitted through such systems as the telephone and the radio or television, and spoken by talkers with a great variety of voices and speaking patterns. How should we account for all of this in our studies?

It is apparent that under typical listening conditions we understand some messages more readily than others. What are the differences in the linguistics of such messages, and in what ways do the different linguistics relate to changes in aging speech understanding under the different listening conditions?

Furthermore, what are the factors in aging listeners themselves that account for their increasing difficulties in speech perception? How can such factors (e.g., memory, vigilance, presbycusis, native language in childhood) be included in our studies?

Knowing that the rate of aging becomes increasingly disparate from the middle years on, how should this influence our study design? That is, if the variances in performance are large (as they often are in studies of aging behavior), how can we reduce the probability that our results represent only the one or so samples drawn?

And finally, should our studies of aging be horizontal (i.e., of population samples drawn from successively older age groupings) or longitudinal (i.e., following a selected sample or more of subjects as they age through the years)—or should we design some other paradigm?

These and other design problems must be carefully considered before undertaking studies with the probability of developing new information about the factor of aging in the perception of speech.

The experimental studies included in this section were organized with such problems in mind, although both the intensiveness and the extensiveness of our efforts clearly have been limited. It is hoped, however, that these reports will provide useful knowledge and will stimulate others to join in the efforts to probe the dynamics of this essential aspect of human aging behavior and to develop effective preventive and compensatory approaches.

POPULATION SAMPLING

As in other behavioral studies of aging, the variables related to different population samples must be considered in the investigation of aging speech perception. Results obtained from older subjects repeatedly show considerably greater variation than those from young adults. Since, in addition to constitutional aging differences, older subjects have been sub-jected to many more influences, both weakening (e.g., noise exposure) and strengthening (e.g., effects of repeated practice), it is apparent that different population samples of older *Ss* of similar ages can be expected to show more varied results than those representing younger age groups.

AUDIOMETRIC CRITERIA

A fundamental challenge to be confronted is the decision of whether the older subjects of a study should be relatively "normal" in their sen-sorium, that is, having hearing that meets the standard criteria represent-ing healthy young adults, or whether they should have hearing more typi-cal of their age. As an example of the former, Antonelli (1970) required essentially normal hearing (average thresholds of 10 dB from 125 through 1000 Hz, 15 dB at 2000 Hz, 20 dB at 4000 Hz, and 35 dB at 8000 Hz) in his subjects. Kirikae (1969) studied only those older subjects (ages 50–70) whose thresholds were no worse than 10 dB at 250, 500, and 1000 Hz, and still found more impaired discrimination of Japanese monosyllables de-livered through a low-pass filter (1200 Hz) than in younger subjects, even though the latter had moderate sensory hearing losses.

Carhart and Nicholls (1971) included those subjects whose speech reception thresholds were better than 50 dB sound pressure level (SPL) in the better ear, while the mean spondee thresholds were only 10 dB worse than their control group of young adults. An extremely relaxed criterion of acceptability for aging studies is typified by that of Feldman and Reger (1967), who selected subjects who had "no history of ear disease," even through their experimental group of older *Ss* had typical audiograms for presbycusis at mid- and high frequencies.

Whereas the audiometric standards for normal, healthy hearing have now been almost universally agreed upon (International Standards Organization, 1975), there is much disagreement on aging curves of hear-ing, mostly because of population differences, as discussed in Chapter 3.

We favor the view that studies of age-related changes in such com-plex auditory behavior as the understanding of degraded speech should start from an acceptance of the decreased sensitivity of the peripheral auditory system with aging. How much hearing loss to include in an inves-tigator's definition of normal sensitivity for a particular age group must, at this stage, be arbitrary. It can be readily demonstrated, however, that an arbitrary cut-off of "within acceptable limits of representative hearing for the age" can affect the resulting findings. Figure 5.1 illustrates how the relaxation of audiometric criteria at only one key frequency (4000 Hz) in the selection of subjects ages 60–69 can affect the results on tests of

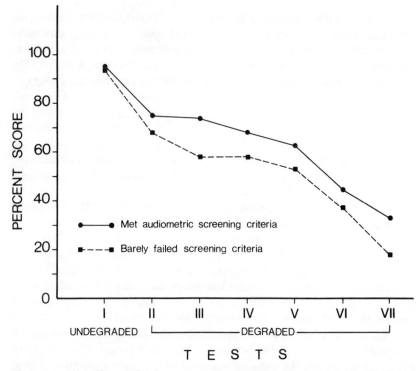

Figure 5.1.   The effect of slightly greater presbycusic hearing loss on the understanding of degraded speech, while the understanding of undegraded speech is unaffected. (II = speeded speech; III = reverberated speech; IV = binaural filtered speech, low pass to one ear, high pass to the other ear; V = selective listening; VI = SSW test; VII = interrupted speech.)

hearing for degraded speech despite no effect on the hearing for unaltered and uncompeted speech.

CLINIC VS. NONCLINIC SUBJECTS

As discussed previously, a relatively common approach in published reports is to draw data retrospectively from the files of audiology clinics (Goetzinger and Rousey, 1959; Harbert, Young, and Menduke, 1966; Jerger, 1973). The subjects surveyed in such clinic file studies almost exclusively were sufficiently concerned about their hearing (or their families were) to visit the clinic. In an attempt to control the factor of hearing loss while studying the hearing for speech in aging adults, Jerger (1973) analyzed some of his data by comparing young with older clinic patients who had hearing that was within 10 dB mean audiometric loss groupings.

Data on clinic patients, however, cannot be considered typical of the larger population of the same age range that does not seek clinic help. This discrepancy between results on clinic vs. nonclinic populations has been documented by various studies. For example, whereas Jerger's 1973 report led him to conclude that there is an exponential decline in hearing for phonetically balanced (PB) words from the 20s through the 80s, Blumenfeld et al. (1969), using the Fairbanks rhyme test on a nonclinic population, found that while there tended to be a decrease in scores with age, the correlations were much higher for the Ss over age 60 than below that age. As noted previously, this finding was supported by Feldman and Reger (1967), who argued that the severe "phonemic regression" described by Gaeth (1948) and supported by Pestalozza and Shore (1955) "is not typical of the aged as a whole, but characterizes that segment of the elderly population seen in the clinical setting."

WHICH AGE PERIODS TO STUDY

A number of the published reports drew population samples that represented older ages either by including only persons over an arbitrary age, usually in the 60s or 70s, or very old subjects (e.g., Luterman, Welsh, and Melrose, 1966, studied Spanish-American War veterans, whose mean age was 84.7 years).

In studies of aging speech perception, however, as in other studies of aging behavior, it is most useful to study *all* decades of adult life rather than just comparing young persons with some selection of older persons. This is particularly important in order to reveal the process and the rate of change and to permit the interpretation of the significance of such change for specific age periods. For example, if decrement in the understanding of speech heard under suboptimal conditions affects persons in their middle years, such as the 40s and 50s, which for many are intensive working years, it may meaningfully influence their working performance. Furthermore, there are so many people in these middle years in the general population that technological design (e.g., of communication equipment) must assign a high priority to their needs and abilities.

SOCIOECONOMIC, LINGUISTIC, AND OTHER BACKGROUND DIFFERENCES

A tempting sampling approach in studies of aging is to test the residents of institutions for the elderly, since they are an appealingly accessible group. This leads to results that may be at great variance with those obtained on persons of similar age but who are living under conditions more representative of the mass of people of that age. Lieberman (1969), writing about behavior of the elderly residing in homes for the elderly, domiciliaries, and nursing homes, noted that "the common sense view that institutions have deleterious effects on the psychological well-being and physical survival of aged adults appears to be supported by a host of empirical studies." It is not at all clear whether this is due to the selection of residents for such institutions or that institutionalization *causes* the serious untoward emotional, intellectual, and motivational decline found in such populations, but it seems to be firmly established that they may thus be distinguished from elderly persons living in the general community.

The institutionalized residents thus represent clearly biased samples, usually yielding lower performance on behavior tests. Therefore, it is recommended that aging studies of speech perception forego such samples in favor of persons living more representative, independent lives.

Another sampling caution relates to the language history of the subjects. As this book shows in considerable detail, if the subjects of research on speech perception are being tested in a language that was not the first one learned, their performances, on the average, will be significantly inferior to those of native talkers of the test language. Although this is apparently true regardless of the age of the subjects or the number of years they have been speaking the test language, there is a compound effect that increases the error further in older subjects. If the object of a study is to note the effects of aging as the single variable, therefore, potential subjects who learned another language first (as babies) should be excluded from the study.

Persons living under different socioeconomic conditions may have or have had dissimilar listening experiences (e.g., quiet vs. noisy neighborhood or job exposures), in addition to those factors that may have intervened in their selection of a neighborhood or geographical area. There may also be psychological and linguistic (e.g., dialect) differences. Sampling, therefore, should be drawn from various living communities, both for the older subjects and for younger *Ss* who serve as the reference for inferences about age-related changes.

The living community factor of sampling was quite forcefully impressed upon us when we conducted a study on the possible effects of the long-term use of a second-learned language on the perception of the first-learned language. Specifically, there are in Israel many expatriate Americans who emigrated to Israel between 25 and 40 years ago, and who use the local language, Hebrew, both in their daily work and in talking with their native-born children. We wondered whether, despite their continued use during a small portion of the day of American English (mostly between husband and wife if both were Americans), there would be some relative decrement in their perception of English under difficult listening conditions. We therefore tested two samples of such subjects, each in a different collective settlement, and compared their results with those obtained previously in the United States with the same English-language recordings applied to native-born Americans of the same age group (50–60 years). Our first comparison, following the study at the first of the two collective settlements, produced the results shown in Figure 5.2A, showing generally poorer scores for the Israeli group. This suggested that there was a deterioration in the perception of their first-learned language, English, after using a second-learned language as the primary means of oral communication for the larger part of their lives. However, when we tested our second sample of former Americans at another collective settlement, the results (Figure 5.2B) yielded *better* scores for this group of Israeli Americans than for the Americans in the United States. In short, the two Israeli samples gave opposite results when compared with those of the American population of the same age. The results do not cast doubt on the age-related effects, since all three groups scored significantly worse than the younger adults originally tested with the same tests in the United States, but they do point up the sampling problems among older populations in different living groupings.

Still another variable in Ss for aging studies is their level of verbal intelligence. Craik (1968), reporting the relative age performance on word recall of lists of words varying from unrelated words that increasingly approximated real English to standard English text, found that the results were dissimilar if the Ss were divided into levels of verbal intelligence. Thus, as seen in Figure 5.3, while younger adults seem to be consistently superior to older Ss in the number of words recalled for each level of approximation to real English, the *relative* inability of older Ss to benefit by increasing redundancy, as the relatedness of the words approach real English meaning, is seen only in those with less verbal intelligence. That is, the age-related decrement in ability to use contextual information occurs in older adults who have relatively low verbal intelligence, but not in older persons with very high verbal intelligence. This finding, in turn, raises the problem of other differences in psychological and physiological function and of social and occupational influences on samples studied. Wherever feasible, the effects of these variables should form part of the studies.

An approach to sampling that requires much initial effort but provides the convenience of repeated studies on various behavioral aspects on the same sample is to assemble a panel of persons representing young, middle age, and old, and the desired variety of socioeconomic status, intelligence, hearing status, personality, and language history, along with

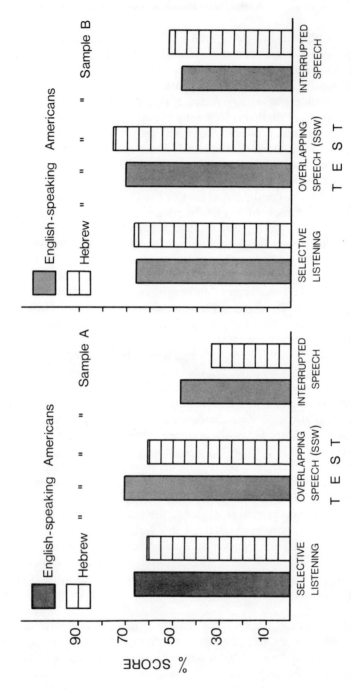

Figure 5.2. Results on English-language degraded speech tests on two population samples of Hebrew-speaking former Americans, compared with results obtained in the United States (labeled English-speaking Americans) on the same test recordings.

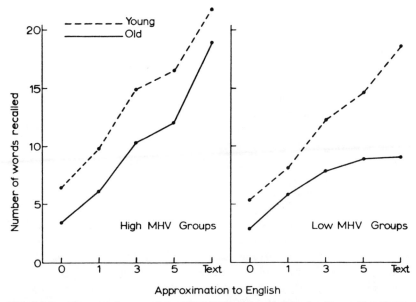

Figure 5.3.   Mean recall scores from 30-word lists of various levels of approximation to meaningful English by two groups of older subjects compared with young adults. MHV, Mill Hill Vocabulary Set B synonyms indication of verbal intelligence. (From F. I. M. Craik, 1968, Short-term memory and the aging process, in G. A. Talland (ed.), *Human Aging and Behavior,* p. 223, Academic Press, New York, with permission.)

the desired proportions of males and females. For a description of the formation of such an experimental group the reader is referred to Heron and Chown (1967).

HORIZONTAL VS. LONGITUDINAL SAMPLING

It is readily apparent that a study that tests persons in various age groupings, such as decades, may not yield the same results as one in which the same subjects are tested repeatedly as they grow older. In the first approach, referred to as cross-sectional, or horizontal, sequences, each younger age grouping will include persons who will not survive into later age. While we do not know whether speech perception and the ability to survive are related, it is clear that with continued existence there are continued experiences that involve a great variety of influences. Gerontologists employ the term *cohort effects* to indicate that persons born in different times have experiences and influences that are peculiar to their generation. This seems to be particularly pertinent to speech listening, which becomes increasingly more electronic and noise-competed and ever-changing linguistically. The cross-sectional approach is therefore more appropriately thought to reveal age *differences*. On the other hand, the longitudinal sequence will reveal age *changes,* but the question arises whether the persons studied over the years are representative of the general aging population even of their own generation. The charge made against the longitudinal approach is that it is selectively biased; that is, its repeated tests attract those who have survived, who tend to be more intelligent, positively motivated and cooperative, less rigid, and physically and mentally well. In addition, their results are thought to be affected by repeated testing (Baltes, 1968; Riegel, 1968; Schaie, 1977). For a comprehensive discussion of sampling problems in aging studies, the reader is referred to Baltes (1968).

Despite the differences enunciated by the foregoing writers, there are reports that indicate closely similar results when both horizontal and longitudinal results are employed in the same study. Thus, Riegel (1968) reported that in data for reaction time in aging, cross-sectional comparisons were "almost perfectly matched by the longitudinal." A longitudinal study of changes in hearing by men reported by Milne (1977) showed the increased rate of change of audiometric sensitivity in those over age 70 compared with those in their 60s, supporting the usual presbycusis findings derived from cross-sectional studies.

Since this aspect of sampling was of considerable interest to us in our studies of aging perception of speech, we carried out 3-year and 7- to 8-year follow-up studies in the United States on selected samples of subjects who had been in our original cross-sectional studies. The results of these follow-ups are presented in details in Chapter 11.

TEST MATERIALS

For speech that is audible to the listener, there are various attributes and conditions that influence its accurate perception. Some of the variables are related to the message and its transmission and others are lodged in the listener himself. Studies of the age-related changes in this most central of human social activities would include, ideally, tests incorporating: 1) representative messages, which are 2) spoken by representative talkers (i.e., age, sex, voice quality, speech patterns, dialects) and are 3) heard under representative listening conditions, and the studies would be carried out on representative age-related samples of the general population.

Few, if any, tests of hearing for speech administered in centers and clinics for the diagnosis of impaired hearing meet these criteria. A major purpose of testing, in such centers, is the differential diagnosis of types of hearing pathology. The tests of hearing for speech are generally those that may confirm the *threshold* of hearing and that will provide a percentage score of discrimination for standardized lists of monosyllabic words for comparison with performance on those lists in known pathologies. Such tests were not originally expected to provide representative samples of everyday performance in speech perception. Despite this, however, there have been a number of published reports of the decline in scores on the clinically employed monosyllabic PB word lists in increasingly older populations. An unfortunate aspect of many of these reports is that they were derived from patients who reported to the diagnostic center with a complaint of a hearing problem rather than from samples of the general population.

MATERIALS FOR SPEECH DISCRIMINATION TESTS

Many years ago the great pioneer in research on speech and hearing, Harvey Fletcher, in a review of the early research efforts at the Bell Telephone Laboratories (Fletcher, 1953, p. v), recalled that one of the most difficult aspects of Bell's investigations was the study of the listener's ability to differentiate sounds that are acoustically very similar. The approach they adopted involved the use of high quality reproducing equipment that could be degraded in performance step by step until listener effects could be noted.

The development of audiology clinics in military centers in World War II first drew upon the Bell Lab's test materials, in the form of sentences, in order to determine the deleterious effects of hearing loss on the understanding of speech. Unfortunately, the Bell Lab sentences were peculiar to facts related to the New York-New Jersey area and were therefore not appropriate for use elsewhere. The development of articulation testing at the Harvard University Psychoacoustic Laboratory during that war introduced the word list approach to the military audiology centers for the determination of the threshold of hearing for speech with two-syllable spondees and for assessing the speech discrimination score for easily audible PB word lists. These two-word hearing tests persist in audiology clinics to this day, and the PB test provides information that is widely familiar and therefore useful for site-of-lesion determination in the diagnosis of ear disease.

Unhappily, these diagnostic tests have been applied almost without challenge to each new development in the interest of audiologists, such as the effects of aging in both hearing-clinic and other populations.

One of the first to report on the decreasing scores, with age, on such speech discrimination tests was Gaeth (1948), who employed the descriptive term *phonemic regression* to indicate the increasing difficulty in distinguishing such single words. The term implies a mis-hearing of the

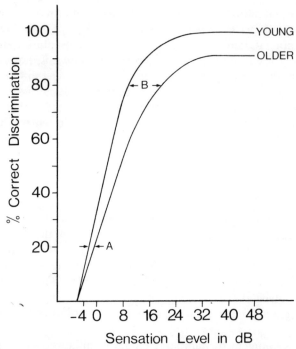

Figure 5.4.   The difference in steepness of P-I discrimination curves in older vs. younger adults is seen by comparing them at points A and B. (Adapted from Tillman and Carhart, 1966.)

phonetic segments of speech that was thought to be more pronounced than the pure tone audiometric changes would suggest and that therefore seemed to implicate age-related changes in higher brain mechanisms. In the mid-1950s, Pestalozza and Shore (1955) supported Gaeth's findings.

The test materials used in studies of aging speech perception have employed, in addition to PB word lists (Harbert et al., 1966; Jerger, 1973; Luterman et al., 1966; Sticht and Gray, 1969), spondees (Carhart and Nicholls, 1971), phoneme discriminations (i.e., testing only one phoneme in each consonant/vowel syllable) (Blumenfeld et al., 1969, using the Fairbanks rhyme test; Smith and Prather, 1971), and sentences (Antonelli, 1970; Bergman, 1971). These materials were sometimes used in new applications; for example, Goetzinger et al. (1961) compared the difference scores obtained on a standard and a more difficult (relatively unclear) recording of PB words for increasingly older *Ss* (ages 60–90), and Katz (1962) used overlapping pairs of spondees in a dichotic competition test. Punch and McConnell (1969) ran PB word list functions on two older groups, one with minimal hearing loss, the other with mild to mod-

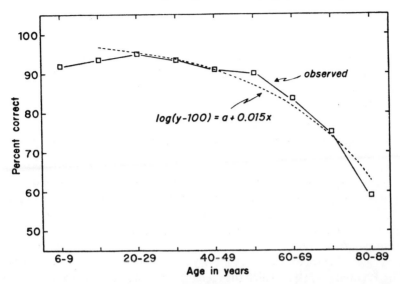

Figure 5.5. Jerger's formulation for the decline, with age, in PB word discrimination scores, compared with the data taken from clinic files. (From J. Jerger, 1973, *Advances in Oto-Rhino-Laryngology 20*, pp. 115–124. Reprinted by permission of S. Karger AG, Basel.)

erate hearing loss, comparing the resultant curves with the normative data for the Central Institute of the Deaf (CID) W-22 lists. They found that the older listeners required higher intensities to achieve scores equivalent to those of the younger subjects. Such comparison of the relationships between percent speech discrimination score and successively raised intensity levels at which the word lists are given, the performance-intensity (P-I) functions, also illustrates the tendency for older adults to show less increase in performance at measured increases in the intensity level than younger adults (Figure 5.4). The steepness of such curves is expressed in the percent improvement in speech discrimination for each decibel rise in the intensity of the speech signal, measured on the most linear portion of the curve. In Figure 5.4 the steepness for the younger subjects was 5.6% per dB, but only 3.4% for the older subjects.

Jerger (1973) published a curve of the maximum scores (taken from the top plateau of curves such as in Figure 5.4) for PB word lists for various age groups, along with a suggested formula for predicting PB maximum scores as a function of age (Figure 5.5). Both Jerger's and Tillman and Carhart's curves are based upon performance by persons known to have presbycusic complaints.

Differences in performance between older and younger patients on the PB types of tests were reported also by Harbert et al. (1966) and Toyoda and Yoshisuke (1969), while Blumenfeld et al. (1969), using the

Fairbanks rhyme test of monosyllabic word lists on a nonclinic population, found that while there was a tendency for the scores to decrease with age, it was only above the age of 60 that the correlations were relatively high. This agrees with the finding by Feldman and Reger (1967), also on a nonclinic population, that the change with age appears only for the oldest age groups.

APPLYING SPEECH-HEARING TESTS TO STUDIES OF AGING

The studies just reported used monosyllabic words as the test material. This is in line with the concentrated interest, among speech scientists as well as clinical audiologists, in phoneme recognition and differentiation. It is clear that this approach can provide us with only limited information about how daily auditory performance changes with aging, however. For example, redundancy often plays a critical role in the understanding of a message. This was shown very clearly in a classic study by Miller, Heise, and Lichten (1951), in which the recognition of a test word was made considerably easier by merely indicating to the subject that it is from a limited number of alternative words or by placing it in a sentence. On a simple level, even multisyllabic words are generally easier to distinguish accurately than monosyllables, and embedding a word in meaningful phrases or sentences reduces the errors still further. In addition, the *grammar* of a language is often crucial to message recognition. An effective measure of speech perception, therefore, would use such redundancies as are inherent in the usual spoken messages.

The use of test words is a tactical error. Riegel (1968), writing on changes in psycholinguistic performance in aging, argued that in language comprehension, relations between items rather than the items to be related should be emphasized. It is common experience that understanding a message often involves rapid error correction of what we thought we just heard but that would not "make sense" in the context of the message. We apparently use our learned linguistic rules of structure (syntax) and our sense of reasonableness of meaning (semantics) to correct our acoustic analysis (phoneme perception). This was nicely demonstrated by Warren (1970), who showed that despite the deletion of a phoneme and its transitional acoustic cues, the listener reports that it is present, and in fact supplies a phoneme for one that is missing, appropriate to the rest of the message. If, therefore, we want to know how aging is accompanied by changes in understanding spoken language, we should attend more to breakdown in response to whole messages rather than concentrate intensely on traditional studies of the perception of small units, such as the test word or syllables. A number of the studies reported in this book support the observation that while aging is often accompanied by losses in hearing for parts of speech, particularly the high frequency phonemes like /f/ and /th/, the decline in the understanding of running speech, particularly under difficult listening conditions, is apparently more related to a failure, in older adults, in what Riegel (1968) refers to as their "information-handling systems."

There are other important aspects of a message that are not considered when small units only are tested. One need simply try to understand the speech of a young deaf child to become aware of the often crucial role played by the prosodic features of speech in either facilitating or defeating the intelligibility of a message. Such children often produce the phonemes at least as accurately as speakers who have a foreign accent, but their speech may remain tantalizingly beyond comprehension. Conversely, the distinctive (phonemic) features can be seriously distorted or virtually destroyed with little adverse effect on understanding. Clearly, our difficulty when listening to a strange dialect of our language, to a foreign accent or to a deaf talker, is related significantly to the violation of our perceptual "set" for prosody and grammar, whereas when these are not strange to us we can quickly "fill in" missing or distorted phonemic information. The important contribution that such additional information in the message makes to the perception of speech is compellingly demonstrated when one is learning a second language, where error correction in understanding depends upon the rise in skill in the linguistics and prosody of the new code.

In brief, it is readily apparent that the clinical presentation of PB and similar word lists, spoken by trained talkers and heard under ideal listening conditions (virtual elimination of competing noise and reverberation in the sound-isolated and treated audiology test chambers) does not meet the needs for assessing activities of daily living auditory performance. At the very least, such assessment should sample the perception of *representative talkers* speaking *representative material* under *representative listening conditions.*

"STRESSING" THE AUDITORY SYSTEM

Given the usual presence of redundancies in a message, what are the factors that expose increasing difficulties in the understanding of speech as we age? As in other studies of aging behavior, in order to reveal reduction of function, one must apply increased pressure to the organ function system under study. In the case of the perception of speech, such stress may be exerted on the central auditory and language processing systems.

Since the central speech processing mechanisms ordinarily thrive on generous amounts of redundancy in speech messages, an inviting way to apply stress to them is to reduce the redundancies. Thus, on the premise that age-related changes in the perception of speech occur significantly *in* these central processing systems, aspects of the signal that depend primarily upon decoding in the *peripheral* mechanism, such as phonemic differentiation, may be deemphasized in favor of tests that manipulate the degrees of redundancy as differences in the amounts of *discernible input*. Such discernible input may, of course, be reduced externally (in the signal itself) or internally by changes in the encoding by the peripheral auditory system (presbycusis) or in the perceptual and cognitive processes.

Alteration of the redundancies of the signal itself offers a convenient method for exposing malfunction in the perceiving system. Bocca and Calearo (1956) began the use of distorted speech to explore the possibility of central pathology in presbycusis, while Goetzinger et al. (1961) were among the first to report the differences in age-related performance on more vs. less difficult test materials. They found that a clear recording of the usual single-word lists failed to reveal significant correlations with age, but the same test lists heard on a "poor" recording did show a positive relationship between decreasing performance and age. Such results and those reported in this book indicate that the effects of aging on the perception of speech are more clearly demonstrated when the listening task is made more difficult. Age-related changes in speech understanding, therefore, cannot be summarized by a single kind of test or test material. The type of material and the conditions under which it is heard critically affect the resulting aging curves. Age-related speech perception should be explored in controlled studies with various materials to reveal how performance is affected by pecularities of the *talker* (e.g., his articulation of phonemes, his voice quality, his prosodic features, such as intonation and stress patterns), of the *listening conditions* (e.g., acoustics of the environment, transmission characteristics if the listening is via a telephone or a hearing aid, the presence of competing speech or noise), and of the *message* (e.g., its vocabularly, syntax, and semantics). An example of the interactions between features of the message and of the listener is seen in our preliminary reports in this book on the relationship between type of syntactic construction and short-term memory. In such a study we found that when a received sentence has a subordinate clause in addition to the main clause, older listeners tend to forget the subordinate clause as they concentrate on the main thought of the sentence. Similarly, the intonation and stress pattern with which the sentence is spoken apparently affect the listener's chunking strategy, which may again be related to memory.

EXPERIMENTAL VARIABLES

The role of learning during a listening session on tests of hearing for degraded speech materials is seen often in the clear improvement of performance after the first few items. Therefore it is helpful, for stability of performance, to introduce practice items first, for each type of message degradation. The question that arises, however, is which of the samples of performance is more revealing of the listener's speech perception for that type of degradation—his initial responses or his more "experienced" responses? Of additional interest might be the amount of exposure required by each listener to "learn" to interpret the difficult pattern. Is the rate of accommodation an increasingly important variable with advancing age?

Another experimental problem that researchers should be aware of when employing distortion as a technique of increasing the difficulty of a test task is the probable interaction between aspects of the signal and characteristics of the distorting system. For example, Pierce and David (1958, p. 197), in a discussion of the effect of different speaker voices on the intelligibility provided by various transmission systems, pointed out that the combination of a talker's voice pitch and formant frequencies with the frequency characteristics of the transmission circuit results in differences in speaker intelligibility through that circuit. It is desirable, therefore, that each experimenter state the conditions and procedures of each study if the results are to be interpreted meaningfully.

TECHNIQUES FOR DEGRADING SPEECH

We prefer the term *degrading* speech to such terms as *reducing the redundancy* or *sensitizing,* since to degrade is simply to reduce in quality. The variety of approaches in the published literature reflect the inventiveness of each investigator. An outline of a number of methods that can be or have been employed for making the understanding of a spoken message more difficult follows:

I.   Deletion of parts
    A.   Intensity. This occurs when the signal is only partially audible.
    B.   Frequency. Filtering may remove either the high or low frequencies, pass only a restricted band of frequencies, or remove only a limited band of frequencies.
    C.   Content. A favorite method is to interrupt the signal periodically or aperiodically, or to compress it by rejoining the remaining content after interruptions have removed some of it. Content may also be removed, of course, by simply deleting parts at the source.
II. Introducing competition
    A.   Requires no response.
        1.   Noise (acoustic masking)
        2.   Other speech ("perceptual" masking)

         3. Other sensory (e.g., visual)
- B. Requires response.
  1. Other speech, requiring recognition, repetition, etc.
  2. Other acoustic, requiring awareness reporting, etc.
  3. Other sensory, requiring recognition, reporting, etc.
- III. Altering temporal characteristics (i.e., speeding or slowing)
- IV. Modifying reception conditions
  - A. Acoustic environment sampling (e.g., varying reverberation time).
  - B. Transmitting media sampling (e.g., via telephone or hearing aid).
- V. Increasing linguistic complexity
  - A. Of vocabulary.
  - B. Of syntax.
  - C. Of semantics.
- VI. Altering the talker characteristics
  - A. Sampling various voice qualities.
  - B. Altering phonemic patterns.
  - C. Altering prosodic patterns.
  - D. Sampling various dialects.
- VII. Altering the message length

It is readily apparent that different methods of degrading the speech message may test different functions of the perceptual process. Increasing the length of the test material, for example, introduces the factor of memory, while other techniques listed here explore such abilities as closure (requiring the listener to supply enough of the deleted material from his centrally stored memories and association to affect synthesis of the message's meaning), selective listening (sometimes referred to as figure-ground discrimination), speed of processing and/or of separating competing meaningful messages, application of deep-seated rules of grammar, and "normalization" of various deviations in speech produced by different talkers. There are, of course, still other perceptual activities that could be studied, such as alertness to speech and sudden changes in the message, and continued vigilance of attention over time.

In brief, phoneme discrimination as tested in word lists may be useful for exposing speech perception changes for very short messages, while test materials of at least sentence length can provide more complete information about the understanding of running speech. The former is useful primarily as a clinical tool, since site-of-lesion information has been developed with its help. For studies of age-related changes in speech understanding, however, the use of message forms that invoke the skills of synthesis as well as analysis and study their interaction give promise of considerably more incisive knowledge.

CHAPTER 6

EXPERIMENTAL STUDIES

CONTENTS

INTRODUCTION TO OUR STUDIES

Miller (1951) summarized in detail his findings, supported later by others, that many variables of speech may be badly disturbed without seriously destroying its intelligibility for the listener. As far as can be discerned, such assurances were apparently based upon the performance of relatively young adults. Because we suspected that the benefits of the high redundancy of speech may not be as great for older listeners, we undertook a series of studies in which the message was impaired in a variety of ways and then applied the resulting test procedures to different age groups of adults. These studies were carried out over a period of years, beginning in the United States in 1965 and continuing, after 1974, in Israel.

Method

The basic method of the studies was to record talkers speaking everyday sentences, then to re-record the spoken sentences through appropriate technological approaches to alter them in various ways or to mix them with competing noises, speech, or reverberation. The test sentences used in the American studies were those that had been developed by a subcommittee of the Committee on Hearing and Bioacoustics (CHABA) of the National Research Council of the National Academy of Sciences. The criteria selected from those specified by CHABA for the construction of our sentences were as follows:

1. The words appear with high frequency in one or more of the well-known word counts of the English language.
2. Proper names and proper nouns are not used.
3. Common nonslang idioms and contractions are used freely.
4. Phonetic loading and "tongue-twisting" are avoided.
5. Redundancy is high.
6. The level of abstraction is low.
7. Grammatical structure varies freely.

The 10 sentences of each list were spoken by five different talkers, varying in accent and including both male and female adults and children, each of whom tried to use natural, spontaneous everyday inflection, speed, and stress. The test tapes were prepared at the Schilling Auditory Research Laboratories in Groton, Connecticut, under the direction of Dr. J. Donald Harris.

A pilot study was carried out on 48 young adults, one-half of whom were noncollege educated and one-half of whom had received some college education, while six older Ss were recruited from a day center for senior citizens. After scores had been obtained for all recorded versions of all proposed tests, final test protocols were structured in order to present easier test lists as practice lists and the more difficult lists as the scored lists for each test condition, since the greatest improvement in performance was seen to occur between the first and second lists tested. With appropriate attention to rotation of test lists among the various test conditions, the test protocols for the field tests included one staggered spondaic word (SSW) test list, one sentence list (CHABA) for the undistorted and uncompeted test condition, and two lists each for the five conditions of degraded speech, one as practice and the other for scoring. All lists were rerecorded from the original recordings to yield peak intensities in the test headphones of 80.0 to 80.9 dB sound pressure level (SPL).

Similar everyday sentences appropriate to the Hebrew language were prepared in Israel, including 10 talkers with a variety of accents representing Ashkenazi (European), Sephardi (Eastern), and sabra (native-born) patterns. Processing of the sentences to incorporate desired alterations and distortions and competing noises and messages was accomplished both in our laboratories in Israel and, under the direction of Professor Harry Levitt, at the Communication Sciences Laboratories at the Graduate Center of the City University of New York.

Another test material used in the American studies was the Katz (1962) SSW test, in which each ear receives a different spondee in an offset sequence, as in the following example:

Right ear: Up stairs
Left ear: Down town

In this example the monosyllable *up* is heard by the right ear first, followed by *stairs* being heard by that ear as *down* is heard by the left ear. Thus *up* and *town* are noncompeting while *stairs* and *down* compete for the listener's attention. The lead monosyllable for each such set of test words is alternated between the right and left ears to balance any advantage that might be related to sequencing patterns.

The processed test material was presented to experimental subjects and matched control groups via easily portable reel-type magnetic tape players (American studies) or cassette-tape players (Israeli studies) through good quality stereo headphones at a level, for most of the studies, of 80 to 81 dB SPL, which is the approximate level of telephone speech production or, as noted, for some studies, somewhat higher.

Because it is not necessary to conduct the test in a sound-protected environment at such comfortably high levels of presentation, most of the testing was conducted in the field, rather than in the laboratory, including the homes of the subjects themselves. This made possible the testing of a large number of persons of various ages who would otherwise not be available to the research staff. Criteria for the inclusion of subjects in the studies required screening tests of hearing, which were accomplished in the same way, through the use of portable audiometers. In some of the studies the subjects' replies to the test sentences were recorded on tape for further analysis and confirmation of scoring.

The use of magnetic tape recordings was helpful in follow-up (longitudinal) studies reported here when, in the United States, 3- and 8-year repeat testing on the same subjects was accomplished with the identical test tapes and playback equipment and headphones used on the initial tests.

Subjects

Because of the reasons enunciated in the discussion of population sampling, indicating that institutionalized older persons perform significantly more poorly on behavioral tests than those who are living independently, none of our subjects either in the United States or in Israel was hospitalized, institutionalized, or chronically ill.

In the United States, our older subjects were drawn from as varied a number of sources as could be arranged, including housing developments in different sections of New York City and immediate surroundings, church groups, members of community centers (such as young men's and young women's associations of different faiths), employees of companies and colleges, and members of organizations for retired persons; many were individual referrals who were tested in their own homes.

In Israel, the older test populations came from collective settlements, such as the kibbutz or moshav, and by individual referral in urban and other noncollective communities, in which case visits were arranged.

In the United States, the younger adult test populations were also drawn from a variety of sources, including extremes of college students and of disadvantaged young persons in job training programs. In Israel there was a similar effort in many of our studies to include young persons who represented a generous spectrum of the population.

Further details specific to each study are given in the many reports included in Chapters 7 through 10.

SUMMARY

The thrust of our studies was to expose age differences in the perception of speech—differences and changes that are not seen unless the aging organism is placed under stress. It may be that the variety of tests developed by us and by others will contribute toward the eventual application of what Rosenblith (1969, p. 15) called "a task hierarchy, a task taxonomy," to press into areas of specific function of the brain in auditory perception. The concurrent accumulation of information from neuro-audiological tests for brain pathology promises to interact with the knowledge emerging from gerontological audiology, to provide new insights into the mysteries of normal auditory behavior as well as its dysfunction. At the very least it is suggested that the study of aging perception of speech can serve as a backdrop against which students of human behavior as well as those specializing in human communication can understand the social behavior of man.

CHAPTER 7

EFFECTS OF PHYSICAL ASPECTS OF THE MESSAGE

CONTENTS

The list of methods for degrading speech suggests the many aspects of the message itself that can affect its intelligibility. As indicated repeatedly in this book, each reduction in the quality of the message, either at its source (the talker) or in its characteristics accumulated as it travels through an environment or a transmitting system, tends to affect older listeners more than younger ones. An important additional variable, previously unstudied, is the *linguistics* of the spoken message, which interacts with the physical characteristics in ways that may permit some badly distorted messages to be understood while, for example, other syntactic forms render difficult relatively clear messages.

Manipulation of the physical and linguistic characteristics of the speech signal is clearly a convenient and accessible approach to the development of an in-depth understanding of aging perception of speech. Much of the following reports and discussion, therefore, is based upon research in which aspects of spoken messages have been systematically altered.

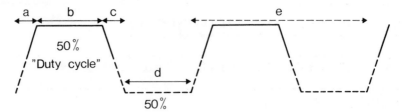

Figure 7.1.   Diagrammatic representation of electronically interrupted speech with a 50% duty cycle: a, rise time; b, on-time; c, fall (decay) time; d, off-time; e, one complete cycle.

EFFECTS OF ALTERATION OF
TEMPORAL FACTORS ON SPEECH PERCEPTION

From observation and reports it is reasonable to postulate that with aging there is a slowing of the auditory processing of speech. There are various ways of studying such a change. For example, Herman, Warren, and Wagener (1977) asked older (ages 60–72) and younger (ages 22–32) adults to localize a train of clicks presented through headphones and varied binaurally so that the right- and left-ear arrival times or amplitude relationships were altered. When the interaural intensity of the clicks was varied, causing an apparent shift of the clicks' position in the head, the two groups of *Ss* localized equally well; but when the lateralization cues were temporal, the older *Ss* needed longer time intervals between the right and left clicks, indicating a decline in their ability to utilize the time information. Herman et al. suggested that since hearing in noisy places depends at least partly on the differential information provided to the brain by the two ears, their results seem to indicate that reduced time-processing ability in older listeners may be involved in their inferior understanding of speech in noise.

Time processing for speech may be tested more directly by: 1) talking more rapidly or more slowly or achieving such speed changes through the technology of compression and expansion, 2) removing portions of the spoken message periodically or aperiodically through electronic means, thus requiring the listener to fill in what is missing, and 3) altering the reverberation time of the acoustics of the listening environment, as in large auditoriums, to study a subject's management of the precedence effect.

Apparently the most effective temporal alteration for exposing age-related changes is interruption of the speech message, with the interrupted portions lost to the listener. This is conveniently accomplished by processing the message through an electronic switch, which permits the selection of an interruption rate per second, a rise and fall time (usually in milliseconds) during which the speech comes on and goes off in each interruption, and the proportion of each interruption cycle in which the speech signal is on, referred to as the duty cycle (see Figure 7.1).

It might be argued that although increasing or decreasing the speed of a message does test the time-processing abilities of the listener, the removal of parts by interruptions is more of a closure than a temporal processing task. That the interrupted message does stress the time-processing ability is seen in the effects of varying the on-time of the signal in each interruption. Our studies on this aspect are reported in this chapter.

THE EFFECT OF INTERRUPTIONS

There are various occasions when we are obliged to fill in parts of a message that have been deleted, either because of the intrusion of bursts of noise or because of the newer technology of multiple message transmission. Licklider and Miller (1951) wrote that "by alternating between two conversations 15 times per second it is possible to provide intelligible two-way communication on a single channel, thereby achieving double use of the communication facilities." An example of the latter is the transatlantic telephone, which could not conceivably provide individual transmission lines for all those who wish to use it at the same time, unless each message was apportioned successive brief time slots intertwined with other messages.

Because of the very favorable redundancy that characterizes most spoken messages, large portions may be removed without destroying understanding. Thus, Miller and Licklider (1950) found that if only 25% of the speech signal is left in such interruptions, 65% of monosyllabic test words can still be discriminated. In fact, they reported that complete destruction of word perception did not occur until 90% of the speech energy had been eliminated. Their results indicate that the critical variable is the percentage of time that the speech is on compared with the silent period in each interruption. As the speech-on proportion is reduced from 75%, the number of interruptions per second (ips) then becomes the next important variable. These effects are shown in Figure 7.2.

Bocca and Calearo (1956) were among the first to report the application of interrupted speech to older persons, noting that their subjects over 75 years of age showed inferior performance to that of young adults. Antonelli (1970) published curves showing the same result, particularly at rates of 5 and 8 ips, and Korsan-Bengsten (1973) reported only a 10% to 20% difference in performance between younger and older (ages 50–60) subjects in Swedish sentences interrupted at a rate of 10 ips, although this difference was increased about 5% when the rate was decreased to 4 ips. It should be noted, however, that she employed one trained male talker, rather than samples of representative talkers. Korsan-Bengsten also cited

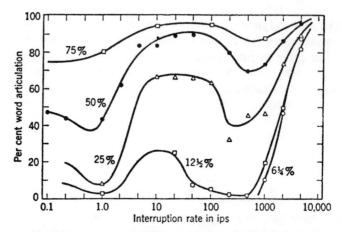

Figure 7.2.   Effects of regularly repeated interruptions upon the intelligibility of words, as a function of the number of interruptions per second and the percentage of time that the speech was left on in each interruption cycle. (From S. S. Stevens (ed.), *Handbook of Experimental Psychology*, p. 1063, ©1951, John Wiley & Sons, New York, with permission.)

Kirikae, Sato, and Shitara (1964) as finding a mean discrimination score of 30% for an ips rate of 5 in subjects ages 50–70.

In view of the variety of results reported on such a test and the compelling evidence the test provides of a central aging process, beginning in the middle years of life, it should be useful to describe our procedures and related rationale in some detail.

In our first studies using interrupted speech we employed a 50% duty cycle, in which the speech was on half of the time and off the other half of the time of each interruption cycle. It seemed useful, in order to allow for a maximum spread of scores from the best to the poorest without a bunching of scores at or near 100%, to structure the test so that the best performance would be close to or less than 80%. Referring to Miller and Licklider's (1950) results it appeared that 10 or slightly less interruptions per second should yield such scores. A sample of young adults was then tested on the everyday sentences with interruption rates of 8, 9, and 10 per second. When 9 and 10 ips yielded *mean* scores of 83% each, they were deemed too easy for some subjects; so 8 ips, for which the mean score was 73%, was selected for the field study. A question may be raised about our use of periodic interruptions, which was technically convenient but perhaps less representative of life situations than random interruptions. Since we were testing with a fixed speech-time fraction (50%), at a known number of interruptions per second (8 ips), we felt that the Miller and Licklider (1950) data on this (p. 169) showed acceptable similarity of results with regular vs. random interruptions. Another concern was the possibility that the obvious on-off transients that accompany such rapid interruption in the action of the earphone diaphragm might be responsible for the poor scores we began to obtain on the older subjects. We therefore compared the results, on samples of subjects over the age of 60, using a 10-msec rise-decay time for each interruption and a rise-decay time of 37.5 msec, which would be expected to introduce fewer transient effects. No significant differences in scores resulted, so the 10-msec rise-decay time with which we had begun our study was continued throughout the field work during the following years, both in the United States and in Israel.

Still another problem in the use of interrupted speech is the learning product of such an unusual listening task. Our preliminary studies indicated that the most marked learning effect occurred between the first and second presentations of the test lists, while only a small additional effect could be seen on the third presentation. All tests that employed the everyday sentences, therefore, included a practice list first, then a test list under identical conditions.

Finally, since the interrupted speech test was given monaurally, the ear under test was rotated so that both the right and left were tested an equal number of times on both practice and test lists, to neutralize any cerebral lateralization effects. Such hemispheric effects might be interesting to pursue as a separate study.

American Study Results

Our first full field study was conducted in the greater New York City area between 1965 and 1968. Of more than 350 subjects tested, 282 were judged to have met our selection criteria. They included population samples in each age decade from age 20 through 89, although some of the subjects included in the 80–89 decade barely missed our audiometric selection criteria. Figure 7.3 shows the results and numbers tested in each age decade. The curve shows the precipitous drop in scores beginning in the 40–49 age decade, and scores drop sharply thereafter until the 70- to 79-year-old subjects, whose scores average about one-third (34.4%) of those of the 20- to 29-year-olds. The remarkable aspect of this curve is its steep, close-to-linear decrement after the 4th decade of life.

Israeli Study Results

In Israel the study population for the three decades 20–29, 50–59, and 61–69 totaled 141 for this test when Hebrew test sentences were employed but with similar interruption rate, duty cycle, and rise-decay characteristics. Figure 7.3 (Israel) shows the results. The decrement in scores for the decade 50–59 is almost identical to that of the United States study

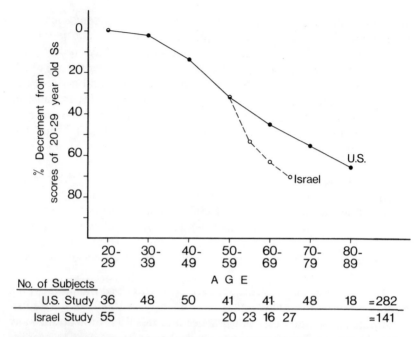

Figure 7.3.   Mean scores by age decades on sentences with periodic interruptions (American and Israeli studies). Intermediate Israeli groups include ages 55–63 and 64–70. Scores for 20-to 29-year-old *Ss* are the reference for each curve.

(30.88% compared with 31.4% for the latter). The next decade, however, shows a far greater drop in performance for the Israelis than for the Americans (63.6% against 44.6%). This may be accounted for by the discrepancy in language background of the older Israelis, since when they were young there was no official Hebrew language spoken in the country and therefore their first "native" language was, in many cases, other than Hebrew. The combined influence of interrupted speech and non-native test language exerts a strong infuence on such tests, as we shall see when the influence of the language background of the listener is discussed in detail.

The startling destruction of understanding for interrupted speech, related to age, challenges interpretation and explanation. Miller and Licklider's (1950) results illustrate that the critical variable in performance on interrupted speech tests, even in young adults, is the percentage of time that the speech is on compared with the silent period in each interruption cycle (see Figure 7.4). As the speech-on proportion is reduced from 75%, the scores at all interruption rates drop significantly. The vertical line superimposed over the original Miller and Licklider curves indicates the

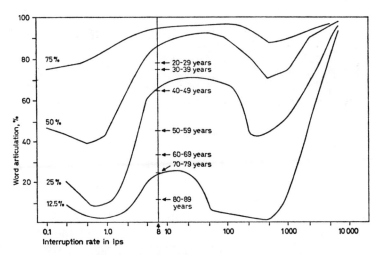

Figure 7.4.   Results of American studies (with a speech on-time of 50%) are shown over the Miller and Licklider curves for the perception of interrupted speech. The decline in scores by Ss of increasing age appears to be similar to a reduction of speech on-time. Percent values are next to each curve. (From M. Bergman, Hearing and aging, *Audiology 10*, pp. 164–171, ©1971, S. Karger AG, Basel, with permission.)

scores obtained in our American study using an interruption rate of 8 ips. That report (Bergman, 1971) suggested that the drop in performance of subjects in successive age decades may be similar to a reduction in speech-on time in young adults. That is, for the same exposure to the speech signal, the older listener may be perceiving only a fraction as much of the signal as the younger listener.

In order to explore this thesis further, a follow-up study was conducted in Israel, in which the variable was the percentage of speech-on time in each interruption cycle. Thirty young adults in their 20s and two groups of older Ss (23 ages 55–63 and 27 ages 64–70) were tested with Hebrew everyday sentences interrupted 10 times per second, at speech-on ratios of 30%, 40%, 50%, 60%, and 70%. This is illustrated in Figure 7.5.

The results may be summarized as follows: 1) There was a large difference in performance between the young and the older Ss at all duty cycles (see Figure 7.6). This was to be expected in view of the earlier results for the single duty cycle at 50%. 2) Whereas at 60% on-time the young Ss reached their approximate maximum performance, the older adults were still far below their maximum at that duty cycle. Since their scores for the 70% on-time were still considerably inferior, it can be assumed that their plateaus would be reached as the on-time proportion reached closer to 100%. 3) On a difficult listening task like this, small improvements in the

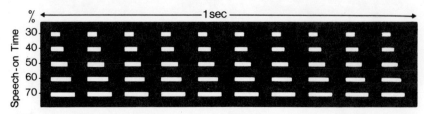

Figure 7.5.   Diagrammatic representation of five duty cycles employed in our studies for an interruption rate of 10 ips. Each clear portion represents the percentage of time the speech was on vs. the off-time (dark areas).

quality of the signal will prove of greatest benefit to the young adult, but will be of increasingly less help at progressively older ages. Note that a change from 30% to 40% on-time resulted in a sizable rise in the scores of the young adults, that a change from 40% to 50% on-time gave the 55- to 63-year-olds their first significant improvement in performance, but that the eldest group showed little advance in their scores until the speech was on at least 60% of the time in each interruption. 4) There were no significant differences in the performances of males and females in the scores of the young adults and only a weak trend toward better female scores in the older groups, where there were 25 Ss of each sex.

In summary of this study, it seems that younger adults utilize the increasing exposure time for dramatic improvements in their understanding of a speech message, but with aging there is progressively less benefit from increases in auditory exposure time, particularly for brief exposure times. This appears to support the thesis proposed by Bergman (1971) that when older listeners hear interrupted speech they perceive and/or process less of it than younger listeners. Fozard et al. (1977), discussing a similar phenomenon in visual perception, reported on several studies that imply that older persons require a longer visual exposure time than young observers to extract the requisite information. They refer to this as an increase, with age, of the "psychological moment," and infer from it that "the number of times that portions of a complex visual display can be sampled for a particular target in a given period of time necessarily decreases."

Discussion

It is interesting to note that as young adults listen to the periodically interrupted speech in these tests they consistently comment that it is "chopped up," which it is. In contrast, in the studies both in the United States and in Israel, the older subjects complained or joked about being asked to respond to a "foreign language." This suggests that when the pattern of the speech message is seriously disturbed, as in the removal of large chunks of it and with the introduction of strange auditory effects (the transients),

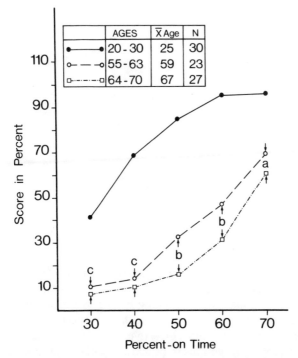

	AGES	X̄ Age	N
●———●	20 - 30	25	30
○— — —○	55 - 63	59	23
□——·——□	64 - 70	67	27

Figure 7.6.   Results on interrupted speech tests at each duty cycle for three age groups. The significances of the differences between the middle-age and the older subjects are shown as: a, 0.01; b, 0.001; c, not significant.

the older listener quickly decides that the unorthodox task is quite unreasonably beyond him. This coincides with other observations in this book and elsewhere (Eisdorfer, Axelrod, and Wilkie, 1963) that once the older subject has decided that the task is difficult, he retreats to omission of response as a corollary of uncertainty. This seems to affect particularly tasks in the time domain.

A word of caution is in order about applying statistical findings derived from groups of subjects to an individual, particularly when age is the main variable. The changes in spread of performance between subjects in each decade is discussed as a major topic in Chapter 10, but it should be noted that even for a task as difficult (scores among some older subjects were zero to a few percent correct) and as frustrating as the interrupted speech test, there are some older persons who perform remarkably well on it. This is consistent with the repeated findings by investigations of phenomena of aging that the variability in deterioration of abilities is seen more starkly as the difficulty of the task is increased.

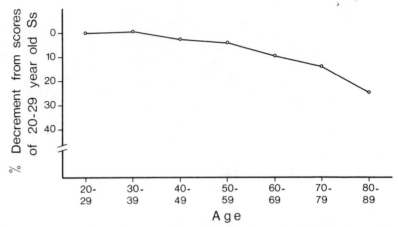

Figure 7.7.   Age decade results on sentences presented at two and a half times faster than normal speed.

A final comment on the interrupted speech test is that it is the most sensitive test of aging speech perception in our experience. The early significant changes, apparently beginning by the age of about 40, and the very sharp decrement in performance with each successive age grouping, mark this test as one of the most effective to reveal age-related changes in auditory perception. It remains to be learned what the neural and/or psychological mechanisms are that account for this phenomenon.

There seem to be parallel aging phenomena in visual perception, as reported by Fozard et al. (1977). They cited findings that subjects in their 50s or older performed more poorly than younger adults on visual closure tasks, particularly for mutilated words. While they do not suggest a neurological explanation for the fact that of all the visual stimuli used in such studies of failure of closure, the verbal revealed the largest age effects, the similarity of results on visual-verbal material and our findings on auditory verbal stimuli may be related to the findings of Brody (1955) that the greatest age-related reduction in neuronal count, in the central nervous system (CNS), is in the area vital to the processing of verbal stimuli—the temporal lobe. Decrement in time processing may also be explained in part by reports of electroencephalogram (EEG) changes with aging, in which there is a gradual reduction in the alpha rate for persons in their 60s, 70s, and 80s compared with young adults (see Chapter 4).

THE EFFECT OF THE SPEED OF SPEECH

It is often thought that older persons have more difficulty following rapid speech than younger listeners. This can be tested by asking them to repeat

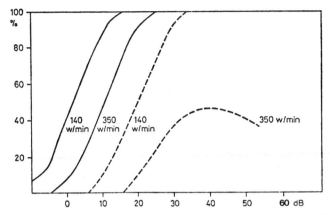

Figure 7.8.   Speech intelligibility scores obtained by Calearo and Lazzaroni (1957) in young and in elderly subjects, when the speed was changed from the normal 140 words/min to two and a half times normal. Solid lines = young; broken line = elderly. (From C. Calearo and A. Lazzaroni, Speech intelligibility in relation to the speed of the message, *Laryngoscope 67*, pp. 410–419, 1957, with permission.)

speech presented at various speeds, either by talking faster or slower or, more elegantly, by processing a test sample of speech through electronic compressors and expanders. These avoid altering one aspect of speech— its frequency characteristics—that may be disturbed in speaking rapidly. They change the total amount of acoustic information, however, since compression discards portions of the speech signal and then compresses the remaining segments together, and expansion repeats segments of the speech, lengthening its total time. Compression therefore effectively "speeds," and expansion "slows," the speech.

In our early studies the everyday sentences were spoken two and a half times faster than the normal 120 words per minute. Figure 7.7 shows the decrement in scores for each age decade compared with the results for the 20- to 29-year-olds. The change in performance was relatively slight, compared with the changes revealed by such unorthodox tasks as the interrupted speech test. Calearo and Lazzaroni (1957), however, testing persons over the age of 70 for comparison with young adults, showed a much more dramatic loss of speech perception for the older persons for a talking rate two and a half times faster than normal speed (see Figure 7.8).

Sticht and Gray (1969) used increasing amounts of compression on lists of individual test words to simulate speeded speech. They tested "young" vs. older adults who met their audiometric criteria of no more than 15 dB hearing level (HL) from 250 through 4000 Hz, and two additional age groups with sensorineural hearing loss, one middle age (average 48 years old), the other averaging 69 years. When they found somewhat

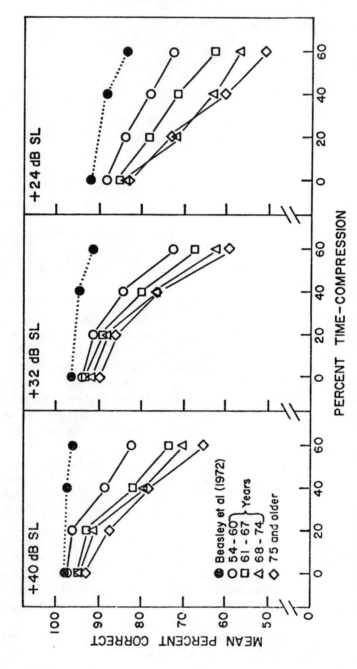

Figure 7.9. Konkle, Beasley, and Bess's (1977) results for four age groups at various conditions of time compression and sensation level. Beasley, Schwimmer, and Rintelmann's (1972) results obtained on young normals are shown for comparison. (From D. Konkle et al., Intelligibility of time-altered speech in relation to chronological aging, *Journal of Speech and Hearing Research 20*, pp. 108–115, 1977, with permission.)

similar differences in performance between the "young" and older subjects in both the normal-hearing and the sensorineurally impaired groups, they suggested that the deterioration with age for time-compressed speech is more central than peripheral.

Konkle, Beasley, and Bess (1977) used the Northwestern University time-compressed NU-6 in a study of 118 Ss in four age groups, with the mean ages of 57, 64, 71, and 78. Figure 7.9 compares the results of their older Ss with those obtained in 1972 by Beasley, Forman, and Rintelmann (+ 40 dB SL) and by Beasley, Schwimmer, and Rintelmann (+ 24 and + 32 dB SL). The older Ss showed sharp decrements, increasing with age, in performance on the compressed single words, as the sensation level of the presentation was lowered and as the amount of compression was increased.

In our Israeli studies we employed an electronic analog of the earlier, rotary-head speech compressor-expander. This instrument, called the Ambichron Pitch Changer, divides the signal into segments; then, in order to speed up the message, it discards part of each segment and joins together the leftover parts. To slow down the message, part of each segment of the signal is repeated, lengthening it. Our test material was compressed to yield a 50% increase in message speed and expanded to produce a 35% slowing of the message. Since the processing of speech through the electronic compressor-expander alters its quality noticeably, the third test rate, which was supposed to be moderate (between the speeded and slowed rates), was similarly processed through the electronic unit. To reduce the linguistic demands on the subjects, we used the familiar token test (DeRenzi and Vignolo, 1962) as the test material, in which instead of making a spoken or written verbal response the subject manually carried out simple commands on small paper forms ("tokens"), such as squares and circles of different colors. The test involves five sections, in which the spoken instructions become increasingly more complex. That is, the units of information increase from three, as in *"Touch* the *red circle"* in Part I, to nine units in later parts, as in *"Put* the *red circle between* the *yellow rectangle and* the *green rectangle."* It has been claimed that the token test results are not dependent upon age after age 15 (Orgass and Poeck, 1966). A study in Israel parallel to the compressed-expanded speech study on young vs. older adults, but with the instructions given live, in standard fashion, without mechanical or electronic processing, found that whereas the young adults scored perfectly, as expected, the normal older adults averaged only 90.1% total score for the test. Our results on the time-altered (compressed and expanded) spoken instructions are seen in Figure 7.10. The young subjects performed about equally at the two extremes of speed, 50% speeded and 35% slowed. It should be noted, however, that

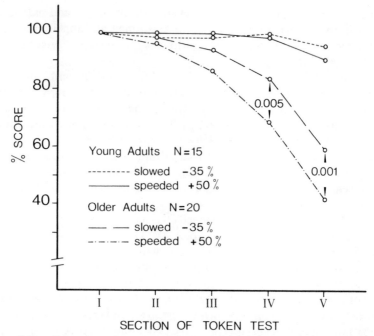

Figure 7.10. Average response scores on time-compressed and expanded token test instructions, young vs. older adults. Significances of the differences between the scores obtained on the older subjects on the slowed and speeded speech are indicated.

on the most complex section of the token test, Part V, even the small reduction of their scores on the speeded version was statistically significant ($p < 0.05$), demonstrating that the test has become clearly stressful by that level. The scores for the older subjects are dramatically inferior to those of the young as the spoken instructions become more complicated (Parts III, IV, and V), and the effects of the rate of speech are increasingly manifest. These results seem to provide additional evidence of decrement, in older persons, of aspects of codification, organization, and storage of complex messages.

The effect of task pacing in older persons has been noted by others. Eisdorfer (1968) found that the performance of older subjects improves appreciably when the pace of the required task is reduced and, conversely, that rapid pacing of a required task increases anxiety, which is accompanied by a loss of efficiency and drive. Using measures of free fatty acid and of heart rate and galvanic skin responses, he demonstrated that older subjects experience more stress under task demands than younger subjects.

Whatever the mechanism responsible for the age-related changes in the perception of speeded speech, it is clear that the major factors are related to central function rather than peripheral auditory changes and are strongly influenced by the complexity of the message's meaning.

EFFECTS OF FREQUENCY CHARACTERISTICS OF THE SIGNAL

For a long time it was assumed that the hearing for speech was fairly well represented by the hearing at the audiometric test tones at 500, 1000, and 2000 Hz, and monetary compensation for loss of hearing from exposure to industrial noise was based upon the audiometric thresholds at those frequencies. There has been widespread concern about the accuracy with which this limited band of frequencies truly reflects the perception of speech, and there has been a consequent movement to include the threshold at 3000 Hz in such calculations, particularly for the determination of the effects of noise-induced hearing loss.

One way to study the relationships between the hearing at various combinations of audiometric frequencies is to ask persons with various audiograms how they hear and understand speech. This can be done in an organized way through the use of appropriately constructed questionnaires, such as that employed by Atherley and Noble (1971). They found that industrial workers showed significantly high coefficients of correlation between their complaints of the distortion of received speech and their hearing at frequency combinations that included—in addition to 500 Hz—1000 and 2000 Hz, and 3000 and 4000 Hz. The correlation was even better when the thresholds at 3000, 4000, and 6000 Hz were included, whereas the coefficient for the subjective complaints and thresholds at the limited band of 500–2000 Hz was an insignificant 0.187.

Since all of our studies on aging emphasize the increasing burden that distortion places upon the perception of speech, it seemed appropriate to explore the relative beneficial effects of including increasingly higher frequencies on older persons compared with younger listeners. Published studies of the relationship between the frequency bandwidth of speech and its intelligibility have been developed mainly around word lists rather than sentences or continuous speech. In a much-referred-to early study, French and Steinberg (1947) employed filters that passed along to the listener only those frequencies *lower* than a specified cutoff frequency (such filters are called low-pass) and others that passed along only those higher than specified cutoff frequencies (high-pass). They developed curves showing the relationships between various low- and high-pass filtering and the resultant intelligibility scores for consonant-vowel-consonant syllables for normal listeners. They found, for example, that as the low-pass cutoff frequency was reduced from 7000 Hz to 1950 Hz (thereby passing only frequencies below that), the average discrimination score dropped from 98% to 69%.

Miller (1951) found that if only the frequencies above 300 Hz and below 3000 Hz were passed, there would be little effect on the intelligibility of test words. Pierce and David (1958) published superimposed low-pass and high-pass curves showing the exchange between cutoff frequency and percent intelligibility for words. The critical frequency below which (low-pass) and above which (high-pass) word intelligibility was equally affected was 1800 Hz, where the score through either high- or low-pass filters was about 67%. The central import of such curves of intelligibility vs. frequency filtering, in planning research studies of speech perception, is the clear evidence that high frequencies are the main carriers of speech intelligibility. That is, the consonants, which are higher in frequency than are the vowels, provide most of the intelligibility.

An interesting conclusion of Pierce and David (1958) was that "a total band of 1500 cps, from, say 400 to 1900 cps, provides reasonable conversational intelligibility in most instances." Until recently, in fact, this concept dominated the thinking behind standards of compensation for noise-induced hearing loss, which was based upon the hearing thresholds for frequencies between 500 and 2000 Hz. The bandwidth of our most widely used transmission system, the telephone, while extending somewhat higher, is effectively limited to the frequencies from 300 to 3200 Hz.

It is of considerable interest to us to test the validity of this concept on older listeners. Is the proclaimed relative unimportance of higher frequencies valid for us as we move through our middle and later years?

Since the frequency area in question seems to be above the previously accepted limits of 500 to 2000 Hz, we carried out studies that passed all frequencies below upper cutoff points around 2000, 2500, 3000, and 3500 Hz. Figure 7.11 shows the results of two such studies. In each study, the reference for the comparative effects of filtering at the various upper frequencies is the performance of the subjects when no filtering was used, that is, when the test speech was presented at its greatest fidelity. The differences in magnitude of results between the two studies can be attributed to differences in equipment (filter and playback characteristics), in test materials (two different languages and sentence constructions), as well as in talkers for the recorded tests and in subjects. Although the filters employed in the two studies were not identical in their cutoff frequencies and rejection rate (the steepness of drop in frequency response above the cutoff frequency), both illustrate the importance of frequencies above 2000 Hz for the perception of speech by older listeners.

Once again, when the task is sufficiently challenging to cause a reduction of performance of the younger subjects, under various experimental conditions, the divergence of performance between the older and younger

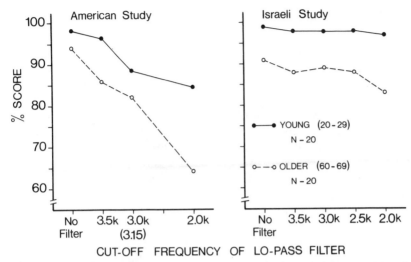

Figure 7.11. Results on frequency-filtered speech tests in the United States and Israel, young vs. older adults. k = kilohertz.

listeners is more obvious than when the task is easier. Thus under the conditions of the American study the age-related effects of eliminating signal energy about 2000 Hz is sharply apparent. In that study it appears that while young adults are not notably affected by a cutoff at 3500 Hz, older listeners are.

In these studies, our older American subjects, who did not have clinically significant hearing problems, showed clear deterioration in their perception of speech when the frequencies above 2000 Hz were filtered out. As the listening conditions became more difficult (even for the younger listeners), the relative deterioration in performance of the older listeners grew more rapidly, demonstrating a clear drop in the understanding of speech when the transmitted frequency band included frequencies up to 2000 Hz, but nothing above that.

It is apparent that any consideration of the acceptable frequency bands for transmitting speech must take into account the ages of the intended listeners, particularly in view of the increasing proportion of older persons in the general population.

EFFECTS OF COMPETING SIGNALS

Everyday listening often involves hearing over a background of undesired competing speech or noises, such as the clatter of dishes, traffic and other transportation noises, office machines in operation, and ringing telephones. It is believed by many that such noise-immersed communication is increasingly a part of our daily life and that advancing technology will bring mixed blessings of convenience and added "noise pollution." If this is a reality of our present and future, its coincidence with the survival of greater numbers of aging people demands that we understand and move to minimize its undesirable effects on their ability to communicate.

Masking of speech communication in noise has aroused the interest of many investigators, with one of the more searching expositions and analyses of current knowledge being provided in a wide-ranging chapter by Kryter (1970, Chapter 2) in his classic book on the effects of noise on man. This work can serve as a provocative guide in designing studies of age-related effects, and its detailed summary of proposed approaches for combating the interference of speech by competing signals contains many ideas that should be considered in an attack on age-related problems.

Speech Intelligibility in Noise

Studies of speech intelligibility in noise as a function of aging have used a variety of noises and test materials. Some related information is contained in reports on subjects with sensorineural hearing loss. Cooper and Cutts (1971), using the clatter of voices, dishes, silverware, and trays in a high school cafeteria as the background, found large ranges and variances in intelligibility scores for word lists in normal-hearing and sensorineurally impaired listeners. Although Cooper and Cutts did not give the ages of the normal group members in the article, their hearing was within 10 dB of normal from 125 to 8000 Hz, suggesting that they were apparently young adults. The impaired listeners included 12 of 15 Ss who were described as "old enough that presbycusis involvement was likely." It is notable that not only were the mean scores of this group lower than those for the normal-hearing Ss at various signal-to-noise (S/N) ratios, but the ranges and standard deviations of their performance were considerably larger. This report and that of Kreul et al. (1968), employing young adult listeners and a shaped broadband noise, note that as the S/N ratio becomes more favorable, the variability in scores by Ss becomes less. Thus, once again it is seen that differences in performance by listeners, whether young or older, emerge more clearly when the listening task is more difficult.

Other investigators who tested nonclinic Ss consistently reported decreased hearing for speech in noise for older adults (Mayer, 1975; Smith and Prather, 1971).

In 1968–1969 we tested 55 nonclinic Ss of increasing age from 27 to 82, using the Fairbanks rhyme test both in quiet and in broadband white noise (Blumenfeld et al., 1969). Our results indicated low correlations with age for both conditions until after age 60, when they were considerably higher but similar for the quiet and noise backgrounds.

The relative disruptive effects of different numbers of talkers in the competing background has engaged the attention of some investigators. Miller (1947) reported that as the competing speech is increased from one or a few talkers to a babble, the listening task becomes more difficult. That is, as the intelligibility of the competing speech disappears, the masking effect is similar to that obtained with wideband white noise.

"Perceptual" Masking

Workers at Northwestern University have been interested in these multiple-talker effects. One of their early reports relating the topic to aging was a paper read in 1971 (Carhart and Nicholls, 1971). They tested 45 older Ss ages 63–88 (mean age 73.6 years) and 10 young adults (mean age 19.9 years) for threshold of hearing for spondees presented in various combinations of one and two talkers and background noise. The latter was a white noise that was modulated to drop below its peak intensity four times each second. The masking combinations were the noise alone, each of the two talkers alone, each of these talkers together with the noise, the two talkers together, then both talkers with the noise. Using the performance of the young adult listeners in the noise condition as the reference performance, they found that single talkers had no appreciable effect in the young subjects, whereas the combination of a single talker plus the noise caused a 4-dB masking effect. They called this "excess" masking beyond the reference effect of the noise alone "perceptual masking," or masking due to the presence of a competing speech signal. When two talkers were included in the background sound, the perceptual masking increased between 7 and 9 dB. By contrast, even a single talker caused a significant shift in the average threshold of the older Ss, although adding noise to the background talker had only slight additional effect. They concluded that "older persons tend to have reduced capacity for handling those complex listening situations that include speech."

During 1966–1968, as part of our study of 282 subjects in successive adult age decades, we presented the recorded everyday (CID) sentences spoken by a male talker in the presence of two competing females talkers reading newspaper stories at an S/N level of − 5 dB. The results (Figure 7.12) show increasing age effects compared to the scores for the same listeners on the uncompeted and undistorted control test. It should be noted that the talker of the prime message in this study had better than average voice and speech patterns, in contrast to those used in the control test recording, where the 10 sentences of the test list were spoken by various talkers, male and female, children and adults, and varied in accent. The differences in results due to age, therefore, are probably less than if the prime talkers in the two tests were the same.

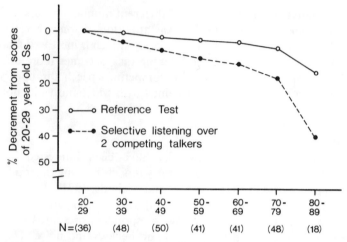

Figure 7.12. Age decade results on a selective listening test compared with the results on an undegraded test for the same test sentences. Scores for the 20- to 29-year-old *Ss* were arbitrarily designated as zero to show succeeding age decrements.

Urban Noise Study

Several years ago an urban environmental protection agency in the United States asked for a study of the effects of city noises, such as from traffic and subway, on the speech perception of its citizens (Levitt, Mayer, and Bergman, 1975). It was evident that this study could not rely on previous publications of the understanding of speech in noise if its purpose was to expose the relationships between those particular noises and the population of that city. For one thing, previous related studies usually were derived from tests of young adults who had good hearing and whose perceptual skills were at their maximum in life. It was believed that this would not reflect the effects of noise on a large part of the city's population.

In order to test representative samples of subjects from the city's general population, 700 persons were screened, to yield 160 in a balanced design of 32 in each of five decades, from 20 to 69 years of age.

Similarly, the talkers who spoke the test sentences on magnetic tape recordings were selected to represent commonly heard accents of that city and included both males and females.

The noises judged to be pervasively disturbing in that city were transportation sounds, particularly from large buses, and subway noises. Accordingly, four noise samples were recorded and used in the study; one recorded in the interior of a subway car as the train ran at steady speed, a similar one with the brakes squealing, automobile traffic sounds, and the

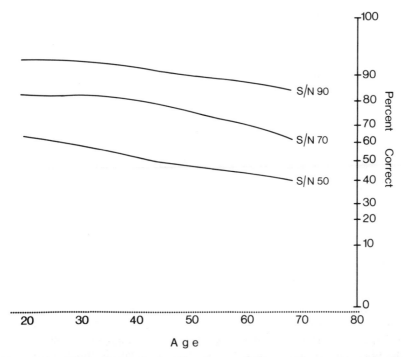

Figure 7.13.   Effects of subway and traffic noises on speech perception at various ages. S/N is the speech-to-noise ratio that permitted the young *Ss* to score 90% (top curve) while the S/N 70 and S/N 50 resulted in average scores of 70% and 50% for the young *Ss*, as a reference against which to judge the changes with aging.

noises of heavy vehicles, such as trucks and buses. These were presented at an average level of 85 dBA and were adjusted to yield an average intelligibility score of 70% in the young adult *Ss*. Additional aging studies employed S/N ratios that gave approximately 90% and 50%, respectively, as the average scores for the 20- to 29-year-old listeners. In order to see whether such real-life noises can be simulated in the laboratory, to simplify other studies by reducing the fluctuations in levels inherent in such life situation noises, the ⅓-octave band spectra of the recorded noises were followed in shaping a generated Gaussian noise through a multifilter. The results indicated the feasibility of this approach by failing to show different effects for the laboratory and the real noises.

Once more, aging was shown to be accompanied by a decrease in the understanding of speech heard under unfavorable conditions. Figure 7.13 shows the decline over the age decades. When the noise was relatively weak (the 90% level for young *Ss*), the decrement in performance averaged only about 6% from age 20 to age 69, with little drop until the age of

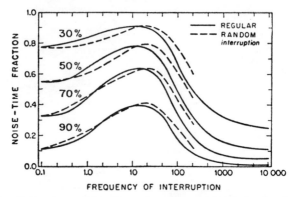

Figure 7.14. Comparison of the effects of random and regularly spaced masking noise interruptions of speech for a fixed S/N ratio (– 9 dB). Each curve represents the combinations of number of interruptions per second and time ratio of each burst of noise to unmasked time, which yield speech understanding scores in percent as shown. (From G. A. Miller and J. C. R. Licklider, *Journal of the Acoustical Society of America 22*, p. 172, ©1950, with permission.)

40, followed by a slow decrease to age 70. When the noise was somewhat stronger, so that the younger *Ss* understood only about 70% of the test sentences, the differences between the 20- and 70-year-old *Ss* averaged about 20%, with a clear drop beginning at about 38 years of age. When the noise level was increased to where the younger listeners understood only about one-half of the test material, the drop in performance began in the mid-20s.

Another part of this study included a test that employed a closed-set monosyllabic word test designed to reveal the discrimination of phonemes (Mitchell, 1973). Such a test places greater stress on the spectral structure of the speech signal and, as expected, revealed greater differences in the effect of different noises on the intelligibility scores than the sentence test material, but because of the linguistic redundancies and constraints of the latter, the results yielded by them are probably closer to conversational reality.

The findings of this study reaffirm that: 1) the intelligibility of speech in noise is reduced significantly with advancing age, 2) this occurs over a wide range of noise conditions and speech-to-noise ratios, and 3) the age-related effect becomes more pronounced as the difficulty of the listening conditions increases.

THE EFFECT OF INTERMITTENT MASKING

Masking noises usually are random in time pattern as well as in intensity level. Since it would be difficult to duplicate closely various real-life com-

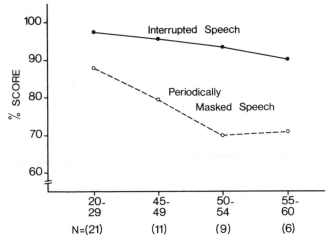

Figure 7.15.   Relative disruptive effects of periodic bursts of babble noise and silent inter-ruptions (each 10/sec) as a function of age (abscissa).

peting signals in controlled tests of their effects on aging spech percep-tion, it is useful to refer to Miller and Licklider's (1950) pioneering studies, in which they found that there were no significant differences re-sulting from random or regularly spaced bursts of noise (Figure 7.14). We were interested in exploring whether the interruption of speech by bursts of noise would affect aging speech perception differently from interrup-tions in which quiet intervals alternate with the message, the effects of which are reported in detail earlier in this chapter. We filled the periods of interruption with speech babble at an S/N ratio of − 10 and presented the everyday test sentences, at a noise-babble time fraction of 0.5, to 21 adults in their 20s and 26 adults ages 45–60. The results suggest that periodic masking is more disruptive of speech perception in both young and older listeners, and, once again, when the young listeners score more poorly on a test, the older Ss have increasingly disproportionate difficulties with it (Figure 7.15). The finding of greater difficulty in noise-filled interrup-tions in young listeners agrees generally with the curves provided by Miller and Licklider (1950) for comparing quiet and a − 9 dB S/N ratio, in the interruption intervals, and 10 ips.

   In addition to these general findings, based on listeners with good hearing for their age and listening to their native language, our various studies reported throughout this book emphasized that hearing loss, such as that from presbycusis, and listening to a language other than that first learned as a young child, impose significant further burdens on the under-standing of speech in noise as one ages.

THE EFFECT OF THE ACOUSTICS OF THE LISTENING ENVIRONMENT

A common situation in which older listeners experience considerable difficulty in understanding speech is in large halls, such as a church, in which the reverberation characteristics are relatively unfavorable for intelligibility. This problem was investigated in 1958 by Schubert, who presented test syllables mixed electronically with various amounts of the same syllables reverberated in a reverberation time of 5 sec, changing the relative intensities of the reverberated and nonreverberated syllables. (Reverberation time (RT) is the time that elapses as a steady-state sound drops 60 dB in intensity after the source has stopped.) His results showed progressive age-related deterioration in the understanding of reverberated speech.

Others have studied the effect of various RT values on speech perception in normal listeners, in those with sensorineural hearing loss, and when the signal was transmitted through hearing aids (Moncur and Dirks, 1967; Nábělek and Pickett, 1974a, b). Those studies employed lists of isolated test words as the signal. The reported results indicated that as the RT is increased upward from 0.3 sec for normally hearing young adults, performance was progressively lowered. When competing messages were introduced into the listening room, the scores were lowered still further.

We employed the highly redundant everyday sentences to test the same 282 subjects of the various age decades referred to previously for the interrupted speech tests, with the test material recorded to provide a reverberation time of 2½ sec. Figure 7.16 shows that this was only mildly unfavorable for the young adult *Ss* who achieved an average score of over 92%. The age-related decrement, however, was greater than that for the speeded speech, noted earlier.

A procedure suggested here for evaluating the significance of the aging changes on this test involves reference to a system called the articulation index (AI), devised to compare the relative characteristics of various speech transmission systems. The AI indicates, for a given speech reproduction system and noise condition, "the effective proportion of the normal speech signal that is available to a listener" for intelligibility (ANSI, 1969, p. 6).

The relationship between the AI and the understanding of sentences heard for the first time, that is, without prior exposure to them, is shown in Figure 7.17A, which also shows that if the sentences were previously known the listener would understand them well even if less of the signal (smaller AI) were available to him, while for isolated words it would be necessary to provide considerably more of the signal (higher AI) before

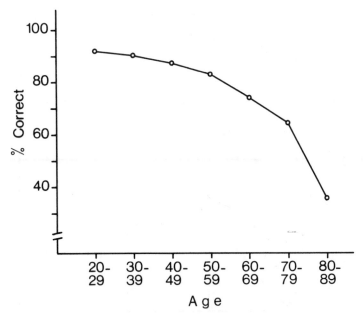

Figure 7.16.   Age decade results in understanding of test sentences heard in a reverberation time of 2½ sec. Total *N* of subjects = 282.

the listener would understand them adequately. The average scores achieved by our 20- 29-, 60- 69-, and 80- 89-year-old *Ss* on the sentences in our reverberated speech test are indicated in the figure, suggesting that under given listening conditions, increasingly older listeners utilize progressively less of the signal and therefore understand less of the message.

If we wish to see the relative effect of room reverberation on listeners of different ages, we first calculate the difference in AI values derived from Figure 7.17A. Since the AI value for the 20-year-old *Ss* is approximately 0.39 and for the 60-year-old *Ss* is 0.28, the difference is 0.11. The difference between the AI values for the 20- and the 80-year-old *Ss* is 0.22. Referring now to Figure 7.17B we locate the normal correction factor (0.3) for the 2½-sec reverberation time used in our study and place our 20-year mark there. Then we place our markers for the 60- and 80-year-old *Ss* according to the AI differences derived previously.

Thus we see that a 2½-sec reverberation time, which permits young adults to understand most of a message, is like a 3¼-sec RT for the 60-year-olds and like a 4¼-sec RT for the 80-year-olds. In other words, what is a relatively favorable listening environment for a young adult constitutes increasingly unfavorable room acoustics for aging listeners.

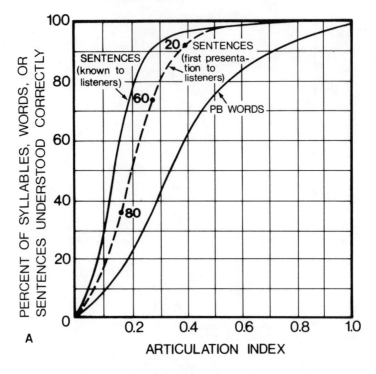

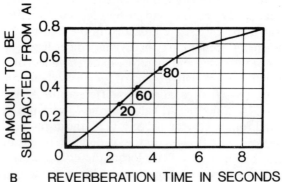

Figure 7.17.   Comparison of scores on spoken sentences by three age groups: 20–29 (shown as 20), 60–69 (shown as 60), and 80–89 (shown as 80) for a 2½-sec reverberation time, as explained in text.

EFFECTS OF CHARACTERISTICS OF TRANSMISSION SYSTEMS

Hearing through the Telephone

Older persons frequently experience difficulty in discriminating speech over the telephone, particularly in the presence of room noise. This is ap-

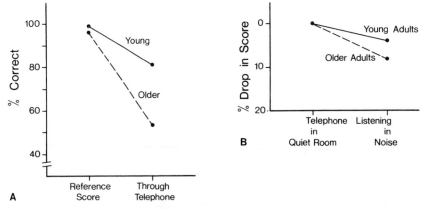

Figure 7.18.   A, Age comparison of understanding of speech through the telephone for a variety of talkers, including difficult-to-understand, compared with performance by the same *Ss* on the same test sentences heard through a high fidelity system. B, Relative effects in telephone listening, young vs. older *Ss,* when a competing babble of talkers is present in the listening room.

parently related to some of the characteristics of the telephone itself and the fact that its use involves monaural hearing. The frequency range passed by the telephone is considerably narrower than in live presentation. In addition, there are frequently extraneous noises mixed with the speech signal, such as crosstalk, crackling noises, and background sounds originating at the talker's end. Of perhaps greatest annoyance is competing noise in the room in which the listener is trying to hear the telephone conversation. Such noises are applied not only to the uncovered ear of the listener, but are picked up by the listener's microphone and fed back into his receiver along with the incoming message.

To compensate for the monaural listening in a limited frequency band, the sound pressure level (SPL) of telephone speech is approximately 81 dB, which is higher than that of normal conversational speech (about 60–65 dB SPL).

We carried out several brief studies of the effects of telephone transmission and its listening conditions on older listeners compared with younger adult listeners.

In a limited study of 16 young adults (ages 20–29) and 16 older adults (ages 60–75), a recording of the everyday sentences spoken by five different talkers, including young, difficult-to-understand children, was piped through a standard telephone line. The percentage score achieved through this telephone channel and telephone headset was compared with scores for the same material heard through a higher quality audiometer system on the same ear. The results are seen in Figure 7.18A. Despite the similarity of performance in both the young and older adult subjects on the control (nontelephone) test for the recorded test sentences, the differential effect through the telephone system is very clear. Both groups suffer some loss in discrimination via the telephone for the variety of voices on the test recording, but the older adults suffered an average loss of 43% compared with only a 17% drop in the younger adults.

When the same Ss listened to similar test sentences over the telephone while a babble of talkers was introduced into the other ear, the proportionate drop in the understanding of the test material was clearly greater by the older listeners (Figure 7.18B).

In another study, in which were added the effects of listening room babble, the Fairbanks rhyme test word lists were spoken to 25 older adults from age 50 to 76 (mean age 65.8) through a telephone line that originated at the research laboratory, proceeded through the central office of the local telephone system in Bronx, New York, and returned to the test site, where they were then recorded onto magnetic tape. This telephone loop, which was leased from the telephone company for the purpose, thus provided the limited bandwidth and other characteristics of average intra-city transmission. The recording was presented to the subject monaurally through a standard telephone headset, first in a quiet environment, then in the presence of a loudspeaker presentation of a recording of a man and woman reading newspaper articles while a radio played music, introduced into the test chamber at an intensity level of 70 dB SPL measured at the subject's head position. The level of the test words through the telephone at the listener's ear was approximately 83 dB, standard for such listening.

Scores obtained through the telephone loop were compared with the performance for the same subjects through a typical monaural audiometer system. The rhyme test in these studies was administered as an open-set test, in which there was no cue sheet available to the subject. That is, the subject was not provided with a printed set of alternatives, such as hot, got, rot, but had to respond to the test word (e.g., hot) without other clues.

The mean score for the control (audiometer) test on this population sample was 91%, which dropped to 79.5% through the telephone when the test room was quiet, and then to 65.5% when the competing speech was introduced to the listening chamber. The differences were significant beyond the 0.0005 level of confidence.

An extension of this study compared the performance of two older groups, one of 12 subjects ranging in age from 43 to 58 (mean 52), the other of 19 subjects ranging in age from 60 to 76 (mean 73). The sharp divergence in performance for these chronologically contiguous older groups appeared clearly when the competing speech was introduced into the listening room as they listened to the test speech over the telephone

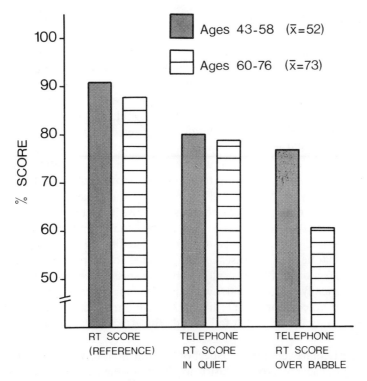

Figure 7.19.   Comparison of middle-age and older adults in telephone listening for lists of rhyme test words under conditions of quiet and competing babble noise in the listening room.

(see Figure 7.19). The disruption of understanding speech over the telephone by other talkers in the listening room, while causing a drop of no more than 8% in all but one subject of the middle-age group, resulted in marked deterioration of performance (10% or more) in 14 of the 19 older subjects, with drops in score of 36%, 56%, and even 84%.

The findings in these studies support the frequent complaint of older persons that they have difficulty understanding over the telephone, particularly when there are competing noises or others talking in the room, and once again the age-related changes are revealed to be clearly apparent by the decade of the 60s. The results suggest also that the quality of telephone reproduction, while adequate for young adults, places middle-age and older users at increasing disadvantage. Furthermore, in view of the greater selective listening problems experienced by them when there is competing noise in their listening rooms, the alleviation of this common problem by the introduction of a binaural headset should be given serious consideration.

Hearing through a Hearing Aid

All transmission systems introduce at least some distortion to the signal, which is then received by the listener. In the case of the hearing aid, the intended function is not only to *transmit* the speech signal, but also to alter it, mainly through amplification. Usually the hearing aid is required to change the frequency characteristics of the signal, that is, to amplify its components selectively. Often the aid is expected to alter the dynamic range of the signal in order to protect a hearing-impaired person from painful levels. Unfortunately, this provides ample opportunity for other, unhelpful changes or distortions to be presented to the listener. For example, faint sounds, such as /f/ and /t/ in the word *fat,* may be lost because of the inherent noise in the aid or because of noise in the listening environment. Conversely, strong sounds, such as the ā in r*ai*lroad, may overload the hearing aid, causing sudden distortion. The limited frequency range of the typical hearing aid discriminates against some speech sounds but does not affect others, because although some speech phonemes are localized acoustically within a narrow frequency range, others, such as the vowels and voiced consonants like /z/, have energy distributions over a wide range, parts of which fall outside the effective range of the hearing aid.

A particularly disturbing aspect of hearing aid reproduction is the introduction of several types of distortion, one of which is harmonic distortion, in which the instrument generates sounds that are not in the original signal and adds them to the final product. Unfortunately, most of such distortion in hearing aids occurs at low frequencies, where the sounds of speech are strongest to begin with. Such distortion may range, on some hearing aid models, from less than 5%, which is not disturbing, to 40% or even 50% on other models.

Another distortion that interferes with the understanding of speech heard through a hearing aid is intermodulation distortion, in which incoming sounds interact among themselves to produce additional nonrelated noises. A third type of frequent distortion in hearing aids is known as transient distortion and results from the tendency of parts of the instrument to continue to produce sounds for a brief period after they are supposed to end.

Finally, listening with a single hearing aid, as do many older hearing-impaired persons, introduces its own limitations in the type of information sent to the brain for perceptual processing. Even the use of two hearing aids (binaurally) falls short of the normal auditory system's exquisite two-ear processing mechanism.

With such alteration and degradation of the speech signal, it is appropriate to inquire about the effects of such transmission on the percep-

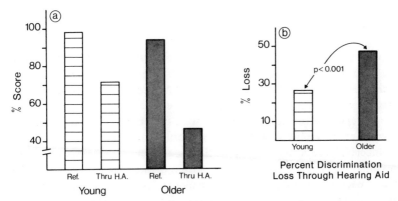

Figure 7.20.   a, Effects on the understanding of speech processed through a hearing aid, young vs. older listeners. b, Same data rearranged to show the relative decrement in understanding suffered by the two groups.

tion of speech, even in the absence of clinically significant loss of hearing by older persons who are, after all, by far the largest consumers of this product.

In a study of 20 young American adults (ages 21 to 29) and 20 older Americans (ages 60 to 74), a relatively high quality hearing aid was used to record the everyday sentences, spoken by 10 different talkers, including adults and children and more than one accent. The hearing aid was placed in a Bruel and Kjaer hearing aid test box, type 4212, where the recorded sentences were fed to it by the test box's loudspeaker "voice" and the hearing aid's resulting output was transferred via a 2-cc acoustic coupler to the input of a high quality tape recorder. The hearing aid-processed speech was thus of relatively better quality than when heard by a hearing aid user since it lacked the interfering acoustic effects of the usual listening environment. The test material for the field study thus consisted of 10 undistorted recorded sentences and 10 similar sentences and talkers that had been recorded through the hearing aid. The study subjects listened to these recordings monaurally through a high quality headphone, with the listening ear randomized among the subjects.

The results of that study are seen in Figure 7.20. The limitations of the hearing aid are seen clearly in the significant drop in performance for both young and older subjects (Figure 7.20a) while the disproportionately greater disruption of speech perception in the older listeners is seen in Figure 7.20b. Since the selection of the older subjects for the study eliminated those with significant presbycusic changes, it is clear that older users of hearing aids apparently suffer the combined effects of their hearing loss and the relationship between aging and the distortions produced by the hearing aids themselves.

Results in studies like those reported depend heavily upon the design of the experiment. The marked results obtained in the American study were evidently related to the nature of the test material, in which some of the recorded talkers (particularly the children) were more difficult to understand than the others and the test sentences were being heard for the first time, with no previous preparatory clues.

A repeat of this study in Israel used a different kind of test material, a rhyme test in Hebrew, and employed only one talker, a male radio announcer. The superior talker plus the use of a closed-set response format, in which the listener was provided with a printed list of six choices from which each test word was to be recognized, made the subject's task considerably easier. As in all studies of the effects of aging on speech perception, an easier experimental task fails to expose age-related differences as effectively as do more demanding tasks. The performance of the young (ages 20–26) adults, in this second study, was almost as good for the hearing aid-processed test material as for the control sentences, and the older subjects (ages 60–80) showed considerably less deterioration for the hearing aid sentences than in the earlier study. The comparative performance for the older Ss, however, even under these more favorable conditions, was significantly worse through the hearing aid than for the control sentences.

Another example of the sharp reduction in the sensitivity of a test when the task is made easier by the introduction of more redundancy occurred when, in a recent study unrelated to hearing aids, we applied the interrupted speech processing to the administration of the token test. In contrast to the poor performance for interrupted speech by older Ss, noted previously, when the recording of everyday sentences spoken by the 10 different talkers was interrupted 10 times per second and with speech-on times as low as 30% and 40%, older listeners had little difficulty in carrying out the recorded simple instructions dealing with the objects (tokens) lying on the table before them.

The conclusion to be drawn from the studies involving hearing through a hearing aid by older vs. young adults is that the electroacoustic limitations of that instrument impose a significant penalty on middle-age and older listeners, even under relatively favorable listening conditions, which is even greater when a variety of talkers must be understood. It is clear, furthermore, that with this unfavorable base related to the age of the listener of hearing through a hearing aid, the added complex receptive problems associated with a sensorineural hearing loss, which is the condition of most older users of hearing aids, raises the level of difficulty of understanding speech considerably.

TALKER CHARACTERISTIC EFFECTS

One of the earliest signs of auditory changes in middle-age and older persons is their relative difficulty in understanding talkers with hoarse or "muffled" voices, with the problem becoming quite marked in the hearing of whispered speech.

The differential effects of talker characteristics on the perception of speech in general have been noted by others. House et al. (1965) searched for an explanation of the different listener results on word lists (the modified rhyme test) spoken by different talkers. They employed two adult male talkers experienced in recording material for listening tests. The listening subjects were 18 young male adults between 18 and 28 years of age. Their scores varied up to about 14% from one talker to the other, as seen in Figure 7.21. When the experimenters analyzed the speech of the two talkers by sound spectrograms, they found that the less intelligible talker's words had greater vowel length than those of the more intelligible talker. They felt that a more appealing explanation, however, was that revealed by graphic level analysis of the relative strengths of the consonants and the vowels produced by each talker. Whereas both talkers' vowels were of equal energy, the less intelligible talker produced consonants that were 2–4 dB weaker than those of the clearer talker. The tentative interpretation was that the greater vowel length combined with the weaker consonants probably resulted in greater intrasyllabic masking of consonants by vowels in the less intelligible talker.

In the perception of sentences, as we have noted before, additional variables enter to differentiate talker effects on the listener's understanding, although it is reasonable to assume interactions among these and the acoustics of phoneme production. Two items in addition to such major aspects as vocabulary, grammar, and dialect peculiarities are the talker's voice power and quality and his prosody (rate, intonation, stress pattern). Information on prosodic influences on age-related speech perception is not yet available.

Talker Voice Quality

While on one hand too strong a vowel-to-consonant intensity ratio can cause masking of the important consonants, a strong voice does give acoustic information to a person with some hearing loss. From this voiced information the listener often can synthesize the meaning of a sentence even when certain consonants are not heard. This is known as "normalizing," or filling in—inferring the appropriate phonemic information. With aging, two important changes occur to reduce the efficiency with

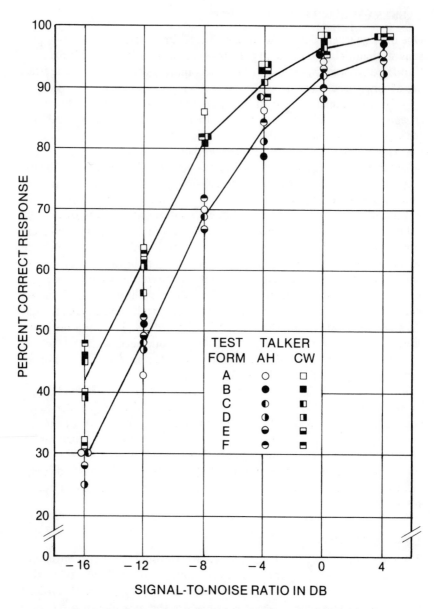

Figure 7.21. Mean percent-correct response for 18 listeners as a function of S/N ratio. Data arranged according to test form and talker, as indicated. The solid lines connect points of mean response at each S/N ratio for each talker. (From A. S. House et al., *Journal of the Acoustical Society of America 37,* p. 161, ©1965, with permission.)

which such compensation takes place. First, there is the widespread incidence of reduced sensitivity, particularly for the frequencies that are inherently weak in energy but high in informational content. In addition, from findings reported in this book and elsewhere, it is suggested that middle-age and older listeners have reduced ability to normalize the wide variety of acoustic patterns for the speech signal, particularly in combination with the changes in their hearing.

Our Studies

In order to document the age-related decrement in the understanding of the speech of talkers with poor voice quality, we compared the performance of young vs. older listeners on test material spoken with different voices.

In our American study we tested 31 persons ages 60–80 and 20 young adults ages 20–29. The older *Ss* included some with hearing threshold shifts as great as 35 dB at 2000 Hz and 60 dB at 4000 Hz, while the young *Ss* all heard within 10 dB from 500 to 4000 Hz. The test material was lists of 50 words each, developed by Mitchell (1973) as a phoneme differentiation test. Examples of items on this test are:

Vowels:	k*ee*p, c*a*t...
Diphthongs:	n*i*ne, t*a*le...
Initial consonants:	*p*ill, *s*ink...
Final consonants:	ro*p*e, loo*s*e...

This permitted, in addition to a general score of discrimination, a distinctive features analysis of the errors made in listening to each talker. The recorded test words were presented at typical telephone level (81 dB SPL at the peaks through high quality "stereo" earphones—Lafayette Model 990). The adult talkers on the recording included one with a voice judged to be a good male voice, one a good female voice, one a hoarse voice, and one a male whisper. Figure 7.22A shows that the young *Ss* of the study had little or no difficulty with the first three voices, whereas the whispered voice evoked only a slight increase in their errors. By contrast, the older listeners gave increasingly erratic responses from the good male talker, to the female talker, to the hoarse voice, and then to the whispered speech. The great number of phoneme reception errors committed by the older listeners was on diphthong discrimination, with fewer errors occurring on initial consonants and still fewer on vowels and final consonants.

Our Israeli study included 20 young adults (ages 20–29) and 40 older adults, divided into two age groups of 20 each: 55–63 and 64–70. Although the female voice was not included in this study, the results generally agreed with those of our American study in that the older listeners

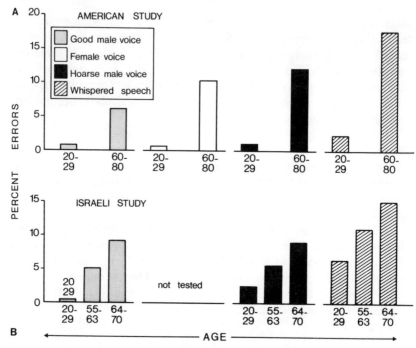

Figure 7.22.   Different talker effects on the understanding of sentences by listeners of different ages, in American (A) and Israeli (B) studies.

performed more poorly than the young *Ss* in their understanding of each test talker, particularly when the talker whispered. Figure 7.22B, representing the results of the Israeli study, shows the increasing effects of age in the perception of words spoken by the three talkers. In this study the older listeners did not have significantly greater difficulty with the hoarse voice than with the good voice. The differences in the results with the two populations studied could be related to differences in hoarse talkers selected for the two studies.

The significantly reduced understanding of whispered speech by both young and older listeners in both studies indicates that the deletion of phonation reduces the phonemic information available in received speech. In line with other findings reported for aging speech perception, such reduction in the external (stimulus-related) redundancy results in proportionately greater difficulty for older than for younger listeners. It should be recalled that the audiometric criteria for the older *Ss* of our studies permitted some loss of hearing, although our subjects were taken from a general, rather than clinical, population. Our experimental population, however, was probably representative of a large body of persons of their age, as indicated by the audiometric curves for presbycusis discussed earlier in this book.

In view of the consistent findings of the age-related decrement in the understanding of interrupted speech and of the speech of different talkers, we undertook to study the combined effects of these two variables on a population of middle-age listeners. We recorded six middle-age talkers—three males and three females—speaking our everyday sentence test items, then processed them electronically for 10 interruptions per second, with a 50% duty cycle. The resulting listener scores ranged from 46.8%, for what was apparently the most difficult talker to understand under such conditions, to 81.5%, for the "best" talker. The highest listener scores favored two of the male talkers, followed by two female talkers. The remaining two talkers were a sister and brother, but even though they occasioned the poorest listener performances, once again the male's voice was more understandable than the female's. The spontaneous remarks of the listeners agreed with their performance scores that the male talkers were easier to understand.

Discussion and Summary

It is clear that middle-age and older listeners have more difficulty than do younger adults in understanding the speech of talkers whose voice and speech patterns are considered poor. Especially troublesome for them is whispered speech. Finally, there seems to be some evidence, particularly from the study with degraded speech, that under difficult listening conditions the speech of male talkers is easier than that of female talkers for middle-age listeners to understand.

The explanation of the findings is apparently in the combination of the characteristics of the different voices and the changes in the auditory systems of the aging listeners. Hoarse voices and whispered speech reduce the amount of information generally obtained from the glottal (phonatory) energy, thus placing additional stress on the role of the resonances (formants) and the consonants, which are higher in frequency and therefore in the frequency region of hearing that often becomes weaker with age. Spectrographic analysis of the voices of those talkers whose readings of the test sentences elicited the poorer responses from the middle-age listeners revealed that their formants were not as clearly separated from each other as in the voices of the better speakers, the periodicity of the phonation was not as apparent, and, in the hoarse voices, the additional tenseness of the vocal cords apparently raised the frequency of the phonation.

CHAPTER 8

LINGUISTIC INFLUENCES

CONTENTS

SENTENCE PERCEPTION

We have discussed the influence of talker characteristics, conditions of transmission and of the listening environment, and certain aspects of the message on speech perception. In this section we examine the influence of various sentence structures, particularly sentence length and complexity, and semantic probability on age-related changes in the understanding of degraded speech.

The main concern is not with the basic strategies and mechanisms of sentence recall. We leave such studies to the linguist. We are interested more directly in those aspects of sentence structure and meaning that distinguish sentence recall by older listeners compared with younger adults.

Sentence Length and Structure

The manipulation of sentence length in studies of aging speech perception implies an interest in the role of short-term memory. It has been shown repeatedly (e.g., Bromley, 1958; Gilbert, 1941) that older persons apparently recall about as long a string of digits, either heard or read, as younger Ss. It seems, however, that this is not an adequate test of older persons' relative ability to recall material that must be manipulated in some way (Craik, 1968, p. 134). Looking at sentence recall as something more than remembering a string of words, it is reasonable to expect that the need to recognize the sentence's syntactic organization and to impute to it an acceptable semantic declaration introduces sufficient manipulation to reveal recall deficits. It follows that the more extensive or unusual the required manipulation, as in complex sentences or long sentences with convoluted meaning, the more significant should be the aging factor.

Since it may be that recall of a sentence is based upon an analysis of the sentence into semantic components with superimposed syntactic corrections (Mehler, 1963), it is suggested that a study of sentence retention vs. aging should look at the effects of sentence length as a *function* of sentence structure.

In designing a study on the differences in the perception of spoken sentences by different populations, it is important to take into account the relative difficulties, in general, of retaining such syntactic forms as the following:

Easiest:	Active affirmative	*John pushed Mary.*
	Passive affirmative	*Mary was pushed by John.*
	Active negative	*John did not push Mary.*
Hardest:	Passive negative	*Mary was not pushed by John.*

Apparently both negatives and passives require a longer time for the listener to process than active affirmatives.

In one of our Israeli studies of the interaction of sentence length and structure, controlling for the relative difficulties of syntactic form, we tested three groups of subjects: 15 young adults (ages 20–29), 15 middle-age (ages 50–59), native-born adults, and 15 older, foreign-born adults of similar ages who had been speaking the test language (Hebrew) for over 30 years and were judged to be fluent in it.

The variables, besides age and language history, were length and complexity of sentences heard. It should be noted, in terms of sentence length, that Hebrew sentences tend to have more ideas expressed in composite words than do English sentences, so that, for example, a three-word Hebrew sentence might translate verbatim into a seven-word English sentence, and a nine-word Hebrew sentence could be, word-for-word, a sixteen-word English sentence, as illustrated in the examples below. The two sentence lengths in our study were of three words and nine words, while the forms of complexity included simple, complex, and compound sentences.

Examples of complex and compound sentences used in our study follow:

Short Compound: We had fun and he was angry.
Number of words: Hebrew—3; English—7

Complex: The watch you bought broke.
Number of words: Hebrew—3; English—5

Long Compound: The book interested me very much and the talk about it in class was very interesting.
Number of words: Hebrew—9; English—16

Complex: The red flowers amazed the guests with their strong red color and with their intoxicating smell.
Number of words: Hebrew—9; English—16

The sentences were presented through earphones in the presence of a babble background at a level 3 dB weaker than the test sentences, that is,

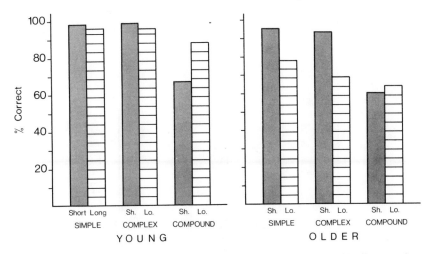

Figure 8.1.   Comparison of auditory sentence perception by young vs. older listeners. Sentence length and structure are the variables.

at a signal-to-noise (S/N) ratio of + 3 dB, to reduce the incidence of 100% performance, thereby sharpening the discriminability of results among subject groups.

Results   Figure 8.1 shows that there was no significant difference due to sentence length in the young *Ss* when the sentence form was either simple or complex, but in the compound sentences they were significantly better on the long sentences than on the short ones. Possible explanations for the latter result are either that the short compound sentence occurs relatively infrequently in Hebrew conversation or, more likely, in a signal-over-noise condition there may be a need for the redundancy that sentences of more than three words provide, since in compound sentences the successive clauses may be distinct from each other, yielding less semantic cohesion than in simple or complex structure.

In the young subjects there was no significant difference in scores for the simple and the complex sentences, regardless of sentence length, but their performance on the compound sentences was significantly poorer ($p < 0.001$) than for either of the other two sentence forms.

Looking at age alone, we note that the performance of the older *Ss* was better for the shorter than for the longer sentences in both the simple and complex forms. This seems to support the role of short-term memory. In the compound sentences the older *Ss* performed about equally on the short and long versions. This is probably because the factors that aided better perception by the young subjects of the longer compound sentences (heard in a noise background) were cancelled out in the older listeners by failure of memory.

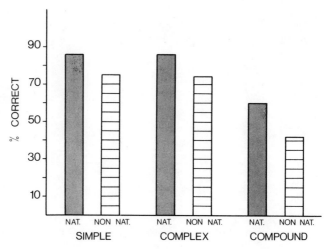

Figure 8.2.   Interrelated effects of aspects of the message and of the language history of the listener in middle-age subjects (ages 50–59).

When the subjects' language history is introduced as a factor (see Figure 8.2), we note that the native-born (sabras) middle-age subjects were better on all three sentence forms than their foreign-born neighbors, particularly on the more difficult (compound) sentence form.

In Figure 8.3 we have charted the relative effects of sentence length and sentence complexity, using for the latter the decrement from scores for the simple sentences to those for the compound sentences. Understanding of compound sentences is apparently vulnerable to the combined detrimental effects of age and second-learned language (solid line in Figure 8.3). That is, the older sabras were worse than the young sabras, and the older, nonsabras were even worse than the native-born, older sabras of the same age. The effect of sentence length, on the other hand, is apparently related primarily to age, as in the broken line, where there is little difference between the native-born and foreign-born older *Ss*, both of whom dropped decidedly more on the longer than on the shorter sentences.

Effects of Relative Clauses

In another Israeli study of the effects of syntactic structure on aging speech perception we employed two types of complex sentences, to be compared with the simple sentence form. Each of the two complex structures included relative clauses in addition to the main clause. In one form the relative clause was of the right branching type, that is, the main clause was followed by the relative clause that qualified part of the main

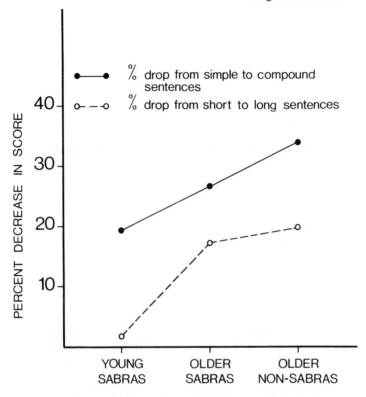

Figure 8.3.   Relative effects of sentence form (simple vs. compound) and length on young listeners and two groups of older listeners distinguished from each other by their language history.

clause. For example, the control sentence in simple form was "The scientist began to teach the young dolphin in the laboratory." (*Note:* The test material was in Hebrew. When translated into English as illustrative examples here there is some unavoidable awkwardness of structure.) The right-branching version was "In the laboratory the scientist taught the dolphin *who played with little children.*" The other complex form was of the centrally embedded type, where the relative clause splits the main clause into two parts, as in "The dolphin, *whom the scientist taught in the laboratory,* played with small children." Sentence lengths were controlled and an attempt was made to neutralize the effect of varying semantics by using reversible subject-object construction, i.e., the subjects and their objects could be reversed without violating semantic acceptability.

The test sentences were presented 12 dB above a babble background, as indicated in a pilot study, to introduce a modicum of difficulty to the task to avoid a "ceiling effect" around 100%. Responses were scored for

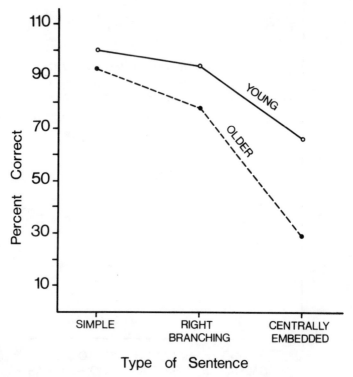

Figure 8.4.   Relative age effects in the understanding of three different linguistic forms of spoken sentences.

correct paraphrasing rather than verbatim repetition, in accordance with the reasoning of Fodor and Garrett (1967) that paraphrase accuracy is an index of processing complexity.

In the scoring, each main grammatical unit, e.g., noun subject, verb object, and noun object, was assigned one point. The simple sentence, therefore, scored 3 points, if correct—one each for subject, verb, and object. Complex sentences, right-branching and centrally embedded, could earn a maximum of 5 points. Omission of adjectives or the substitution of a word by a similar word was allowed without penalty, thereby reducing the memory requirement somewhat but retaining the need to relate subject, verb, and object as the key to sentence processing.

The subjects of the study were 21 young adults (ages 20–29) and 21 older adults (ages 60–70), all of whom were without noticeable hearing problems or complaints.

Results   Figure 8.4 illustrates the increasing difficulty in sentence perception / recall as the structural form becomes more complex, even for the young adults. Once again, as the task becomes more difficult for them, it becomes disproportionately harder for older listeners.

An interesting observation in this study was that the older *Ss* showed a greater tendency than the younger *Ss* to recall only the main clause of the complex sentences. Both groups had greater difficulty recalling the centrally embedded relative clauses compared with recalling the right-branching clauses, which agrees with Slobin's (1971) finding that sentences with interruptions or those that require rearrangement of their linguistic elements present greater difficulties than sentences without such requirements. Our study emphasizes that this difficulty becomes greater with aging.

The tendency of our *Ss* to understand only the main clause in the centrally embedded sentences suggests that they temporarily disregard the relative clause until they have the main idea in mind, but then forget that clause. Such limitations of short-term memory are apparently greater in older persons. In this matter we recall the findings of Inglis and Tansey (1967) in dichotic listening tasks, where *Ss* were required to hold one string of words in memory storage while repeating aloud another string of words that were heard at the same time. In that study there was little difference between young and older *Ss* in the immediate recall of the first string of words to be reported, but increasingly marked decrement, with age, characterized the recall of the string of words from short-term memory.

It is suggested that in complex sentences a similar division of response is made, in which the main clause is processed immediately, with the subordinate clause held at the mercy of short-term memory.

SEMANTIC INFLUENCES

Effects of the Range of Alternatives

Miller (1951) emphasized that a speech articulation score may be as low as 5% or as high as 95% under identical listening conditions, according to the nature of the material of the message. Thus, if the intended message is one of a large number of possible messages, it is less likely to be understood by the listener than if it is one of a small number of alternative possibilities.

A classic study supporting this that has strongly influenced thinking about speech perception is that of Miller, Heise, and Lichten (1951), in which the decision on what is heard was shown to be influenced strongly by the number of possible choices. Thus, if what is heard is one of only two possible words, our recognition performance is very high as long as

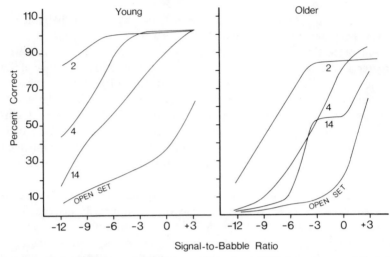

Figure 8.5. Age-related effects of the number of possible alternative words heard at various signal-to-noise ratios.

the test word can be heard even very faintly. If, by contrast, the test word is one of a pool of dozens of possibilities, we need considerably more intensity before we can reply correctly or with certainty.

We were interested in learning whether the decrease in the number of choices in which the test word appears would be as beneficial to older listeners as to younger adults. We therefore replicated the general format of the Miller et al. study, but in Hebrew, and compared the performances of 20 young adults (ages 20–28) with those of 20 older adults (ages 61–70). The two variables in the test included signal-to-babble ratio and number of alternatives from which the test word had to be selected.

Results When the test word was selected from an open set, that is, from a virtually limitless range of possible choices, the performance of the two groups of *Ss* (although the younger *Ss* were generally superior) showed the same relatively poor scores until a critical signal-to-background babble ratio (+ 3) was reached. As soon as the set was limited, however, by a displayed choice of alternatives, it became clear that the younger subjects utilized the increased redundancy far more effectively than the older listeners (see Figure 8.5).

If we replot the results as a function only of the number of alternatives employed in the study and summarize the scores at all S/N ratios, this effect is seen clearly (Figure 8.6). The difference in improvement in the performance of the younger and older *Ss* when the number of possible alternatives is reduced is marked. That is, the increasing redundancy (improved probabilities) provides less benefit for the older listener.

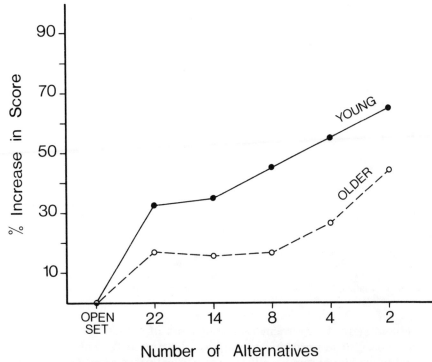

Figure 8.6. Data from Figure 8.5 replotted to provide a common reference point for the open-set scores of the two age populations, illustrating the difference in improvement resulting from fewer alternatives (higher redundancy). Scores for all S/N ratios were consolidated.

The relative effect on the two age groups of the background babble was apparently not as significant a factor in the results of this study as the range of alternatives. Figure 8.7a shows the actual curves derived from the results of each group, and Figure 8.7b superimposes the two curves to show the similarity of growth function with changes in the S/N ratio. This is in agreement with the findings of Smith and Prather (1971).

As noted throughout this book and elsewhere (Craik, 1968, p. 154, Davies, 1968, p. 230), older adults tend to withold responses when they are uncertain rather than risk error. In this study of the effect of alternatives, the older *Ss* accumulated more than six times the number of *omissions* of responses as the younger *Ss*.

In summary of this study, it appears: 1) that the older listeners were consistently worse than the younger listeners at all S/N ratios and at all ranges of alternative choices from which the test word was to be selected, and 2) that as the number of possible alternative choices was systematically reduced, thereby increasing the redundancy, the young listeners

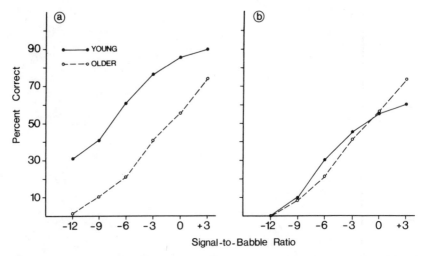

Figure 8.7.   The data from Figure 8.6 for all ranges of alternatives have been consolidated to show the relative effects of signal-to-babble ratios on the young and older listeners (a). In b the overall difference in performance is eliminated by referencing the two curves together at an S/N ratio of − 12 to show the relative growth function as the S/N ratio improves.

showed marked improvement in recognition of the test words, whereas the older listeners experienced significantly less benefit. This relative inability of older persons to utilize clues efficiently is in agreement with the findings of Rabbitt (1968) on visual reaction time, where foresignals did not help older subjects at all but did help the younger subjects. This may be because the older Ss tend to ignore alternatives placed before them, as illustrated by the lag in obtaining improved scores as the range of alternatives is narrowed. A further indication of this is seen in the tendency of some older listeners to supply, and often to insist upon, a *non*-included word despite closed set-limited choices. This has been seen repeatedly in our studies.

Effects of the Levels of Probability

Another approach to the study of the relative efficiency of older listeners in utilizing a heightened level of probability in their perception of speech is provided in the recently introduced Speech Perception in Noise (SPIN) test (Kalikow, Stevens, and Elliott, 1977). We constructed similar materials in Hebrew to contain two levels of predictability, high and low. In the test version only the last word of the sentence is to be repeated by the subject, but each test word appears in two lists of test sentences, in one as a high probability word and in the other as a low probability word. Each list has a mixture of high and low probability sentences. An example of

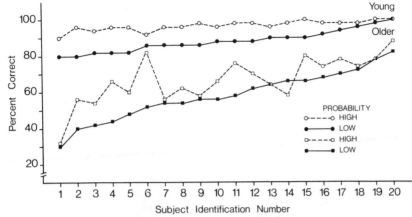

Figure 8.8.   Scores for each young and each older subject on the perception of test words delivered as high or low probability, depending upon clues provided in their carrier sentences. Each subject's two scores (low and high probability) are shown one above the other.

low probability is "Bill was discussing the *bay,*" and an example of the same word in a high probability sentence that includes pointers, or clues, is "The boat sailed across the *bay.*" High probability sentences were developed by the use of a preliminary paper-and-pencil study in which a number of persons were given typed stems of the sentences and were asked to supply each with a word that would be most likely to complete the sentence. Words that occurred a large proportion of the time, but not all of the time, were selected for use with those sentences in the high-probability version.

Twenty young adults (ages 20–26) with normal hearing and 20 older adults (ages 56–82, with a mean age of 69) were tested. All sentences were presented at a comfortably high level in the presence of babble background, which was 4 dB below the level of the speech signal, in order to avoid the ceiling effect of 100% performance.

Results   Figure 8.8 shows the individual scores for each subject, young and older, arranged for clarity from the lowest to the highest for each group. The low probability score for each subject can be considered his basic performance for speech discrimination in noise, and is therefore the control score in relation to which his high probability sentence score illustrates his efficiency in utilizing the clues provided in the latter. Note that in the younger *Ss* the differences in their basic discrimination in noise are almost uniformly overcome (scores around 100%) when contextual clues are provided. When we look at the results of the older *Ss* we note first that the performance for both high and low probability sentences are clearly inferior to that of the younger *Ss* in the presence of background

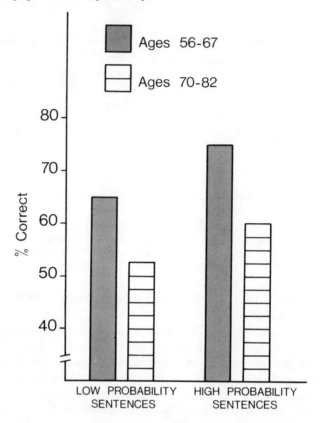

Figure 8.9.   Comparison of the performance on low and high probability sentences by two older populations.

babble, but of special interest here is the great variation among them in the cognitive aspects of their speech perception.

When the older *Ss* in this study are divided into age groups of 56–67 (*N* = 9) and 70–82 (*N* = 11), we see that the eldest group performs lower on both low and high probability sentences than the middle group. The differences are statistically significant. Figure 8.9 compares their mean scores and shows the tendency for the middle group to benefit relatively more than the eldest *Ss* from the clues in the high probability sentences.

The results of these preliminary studies on the effects of semantic probability support earlier observations (Rabbitt, 1968, p. 85) that older persons make less efficient use of linguistic redundancy than the young.

CHAPTER 9

FACTORS IN THE LISTENER THAT AFFECT THE PERCEPTION OF SPEECH

CONTENTS

Auditory perception, whether for speech or other signals, requires certain attributes of the listener. The following is a partial outline of these:

1. Attention
   a. focusing on simple and complex stimuli
   b. sustaining attention (vigilance)
   c. tracking (i.e., following shifts of content and type of signal)
2. Discrimination, of phonemes and prosodic features of speech
3. Memory
   a. short-term storage
   b. long-term storage and recall
4. Message completion ("closure") of:
   a. time-removed material (interrupted by periods of silence or bursts of noise)
   b. intensity-removed material (vowel-dominated consonants)
   c. frequency-removed material (e.g., filtered)

5. Adjustment to time-flow effects
   a. speeded speech
   b. slowed speech
6. Separation/integration of competing messages or parts of a message
   a. interaural perceptual separation (e.g., in dichotic listening)
   b. binaural fusion
   c. selective listening ("figure-ground")

Each listener has personal factors that determine his ability to apply such attributes of auditory perception to the understanding of speech. Some of the more apparent of these factors are: 1) function of peripheral hearing mechanism; 2) disturbances in peripheral encoding; 3) memory, short-term and storage, 4) preferred signal-to-competing noise level for comfortable listening; 5) experience in the language and/or dialect of the talker; 6) cognitive abilities, e.g., utilization of available clues and ability to effect closure (synthesis) when parts of a message are missing; 7) level of motivation and confidence during exposure to a spoken message, the stability of motivation, and positive and negative responses to suggestion; and 8) vigilance, i.e., alertness to changing events about the person and ability to maintain such alertness over time.

For extensive coverage of present knowledge on some of these factors, the reader is referred to writings on the psychological aspects of aging, such as Birren and Schaie (1977) and Talland (1968). In the treatment that follows we report the results of our own studies where applicable.

PERIPHERAL EAR CHANGES

Auditory Sensitivity

The amount and quality of input from the peripheral hearing mechanism to the central nervous system (CNS) has an important influence on the understanding of a message. Thus a factor of interest is the hearing sensitivity for sounds of various frequencies. Until a moderate to moderately severe level of hearing loss occurs for such frequencies as 3000 and 4000 Hz in cases of typical presbycusis, where hearing for the lower and middle frequencies remains good, there is little interference with message perception, although there may be mis-hearing of specific phonemes, such as /s/ and /f/. If, however, the hearing at middle and lower frequencies, such as 1000 and 500 Hz, drops to audiometric levels of about 35 dB or more, there will be a noticeable lack of understanding much of the time.

As we noted in Chapter 3 on presbycusis, there is a fairly high incidence of high-tone hearing loss in later years of life, and in the decades above age 70 we can expect increasing requests for repetition of messages even under favorable listening conditions.

Such hearing problems under good listening conditions do not usually occur to persons younger than 60. As we have seen in other sections of this book, however, there are clear decrements in auditory ability even in middle-age listeners when listening conditions are less favorable. In some persons this may be due to beginning changes in sensitivity of the peripheral mechanism, but it is suspected that the central auditory and processing systems are strongly involved.

Other Cochlear Changes

It is probable that even in the absence of a significant loss of hearing as seen on a pure tone audiogram, cochlear function can change in ways that will distort the encoded signal it sends to the CNS for processing (Hume, 1978; Lipscomb, 1975).

A procedure for revealing such dysfunction is the aural overload test, in which a probe tone, e.g., 1000 Hz, is introduced into the ear along with an exploring tone that is an octave higher plus 3 Hz, which in our example would be 2003 Hz. The exploring tone is kept at a constant 10 dB below the level of the probe tone. At a given intensity level of the probe tone above its threshold of audibility, the listener will hear a beating tone, which will be the result of the 2003-Hz tone mixing with a 2000-Hz tone being generated within the ear as a harmonic of the 1000-Hz probe tone. Preliminary data on the application of this technique to persons of middle age are presented in Chapter 3.

Once normative data have been established for the sensation level (SL) (i.e., the level above threshold for the probe tone) at which such beating begins, dysfunction of the hair cells is deduced from an increase or decrease in such sensation level. Hume (1978) reported preliminary experimental findings relating cochlear dysfunction, as indicated by lowered aural overload thresholds, with poor discrimination of speech in noise, since the hearing is "driven further into the range of nonlinearity."

Unfortunately, because of the need for special equipment not usually available in audiology clinics and the difficulty exhibited by a number of clinical patients in recognizing the existence or absence of a beating tone, the aural overload test has not gained general acceptance. However, it can be a useful tool for the discovery of early, preaudiometric change dysfunction relating to the aging process in the cochlea.

Since peripheral auditory disturbances sufficient to cause changes in hearing for speech under certain conditions can apparently occur even before significant audiometric shifts are seen, it is reasonable to suspect that aging changes begin thus, followed only later by presbycusic audiograms. The relationship between such cochlear changes and speech perception with aging have yet to be studied and reported.

Another approach to the study of the function of the peripheral auditory mechanism either with or without audiometric evidence of change is through Békésy automatic audiometry tracings, in which the testee is required to press a button when he hears a tone (causing the signal to be automatically lowered in intensity) and to release the button when he no longer hears the tone (signaling the audiometer to gradually increase the tone's intensity until it is heard again). Two tracings are usually made in this test, one to a continuous tone, which is gradually rising in frequency, and a similar one to pulsed tones, also of gradually rising frequency, but where each tone is a pip of ½-sec duration followed by a ½-sec pause and then another tone pip. A normal result is to find these two tracings superimposed on each other. In presbycusic cochlear hearing changes for the higher frequencies, however, the tracings are superimposed only for the lower and middle frequencies, but the tracing for the continuous tones falls below (worse hearing) the pulsed tone tracings at the frequencies at which there is some loss of sensitivity.

In our Parkchester research project on aging speech perception we conducted a limited study of older persons to see if there are any unusual Békésy audiograms in such a population. Two measures of their tracings were analyzed: the amplitude of the tracing excursions, from the point indicating the beginning of tone audibility to the point indicating its cessation, and the relationship, or coincidence, of the continuous and pulsed tracings. For the first analysis we tested 30 persons, with a mean age of 64.3, and found that the mean amplitude of their tracing excursions at frequencies of 250, 1000, and 4000 Hz was from two to two and a half times as large as the mean amplitudes reported (Siegenthaler, 1961) for the same attenuation rate of the audiometer for young adults, ages 18–31. The larger amplitudes of the tracing excursions are probably related to increased reaction time in the older subjects. This may not, however, rule out a possible change of function of the cochlea and its associated neural transmission system up to the cortex.

In the second analysis·we noted that there were frequent separations between the pulsed and continuous tone tracings at 250 and 1000 Hz in addition to the anticipated separation, for older Ss, at 4000 Hz. This occurred even in persons whose hearing thresholds at the two lower frequencies were essentially normal. We therefore obtained 53 Békésy tracings at the same three frequencies from subjects ranging in age from 50 to 79, the bulk of whom were between 60 and 69. While these included some Ss with normal thresholds, particularly at 250 Hz, many of them had sensorineural hearing losses, which usually result in smaller than normal excursion amplitudes on the Békésy tracings. The resultant mean differences between the pulsed and continuous tracings were significant at all three test frequencies, in contrast to the fact that in young, normal-hearing adults there are generally no such differences.

These findings on older listeners apparently indicate abnormal function of the peripheral hearing mechanism, probably related to neural adaptation. This in turn can be expected to affect adversely the nature of the input signals for speech that are forwarded to the CNS for processing for meaning.

In brief, the older cochlea generally shows changes in hearing for higher audiometric frequencies, and there is some evidence that other sounds may be abnormally encoded by the peripheral auditory system.

EFFECTS OF THE LISTENER'S LANGUAGE AND DIALECT HISTORY

An unanticipated development in our American investigations in the mid-1960s on aging speech perception emerged late one afternoon when we were reviewing the data collected earlier that day on Ss between the ages of 60 and 69. This was the second population sample we had tested in that age decade and we were puzzled over why the results on the six degraded speech tests were consistently poorer than those we had obtained on the earlier sample. The only reasonable explanation seemed to be that many of the day's Ss had been drawn from a single housing development in New York City and spoke in accented, albeit fluent, English. A follow-up of the subjects the next day revealed that they had been born abroad but had been in the United States and speaking English for an average of over 50 years. Figure 9.1 shows the results of the tests on the two sample groups. While there appears to be only a slight difference in scores on the undistorted control sentences, the divergences of performance on all of the degraded speech tests are clear.

Intrigued by the apparently persisting deficit in speech perception under difficult listening conditions, we carried this study further in Israel, where a large proportion of older residents are not sabras (native-born Israelis). Since Hebrew as the reinstated national language did not take hold universally in modern Israel until relatively recently, it was difficult to find older subjects whose first language was Hebrew, even if they had been born in the country. Even the older (over age 60) sabras of our studies had been greatly exposed to languages other than Hebrew as children.

Because of this we designed many of our aging studies around 50- to 59-year-old subjects. We soon discovered that this was a fortuitous development, since we were able to expose a number of significant age-related changes in speech perception in that middle-age group, thus shifting the

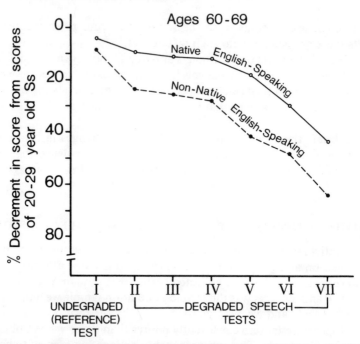

Figure 9.1. Performance of 14 fluent English-speaking older subjects whose first-learned language was not English, compared with native-born speakers of English of the same age decade. The close agreement in scores on the undegraded reference test is contrasted with the clear difference in scores of the various degraded speech tests. (See Figure 5.1 for explanation of the degraded speech tests.)

focus, in our aging studies, from old persons to those who are still at the peak of their involvement in society's activities.

Israeli Studies

Since our American studies revealed very significant age-associated changes in the perception of interrupted speech, we decided to employ that test as well as one other more lifelike test to explore the effect of a non-first-learned language as the test instrument. Accordingly, a selective listening task, involving the perception of a prime message in the presence of a competing background of talkers, was adopted as the second test.

A preliminary study was carried out on young adults between the ages of 20 and 29 to see whether the speech-masked speech perception test would be sensitive to the language background factor in the absence of the aging factor so strongly associated with the interrupted speech test. Eighteen sabras were matched with 12 nonsabras, of similar age, who had spoken another language at least until the age of 7 but who had been speaking Hebrew for at least 13 years and were judged to be fluent in it,

Table 1. Effects of testing in a second-learned language, young adults ages 20–29, native-born talkers of Hebrew vs. non-native born (mean scores)

	N	Undistorted sentences	Speech-masked speech	Interrupted speech
Sabras	18	99.8_a	80_b	93.2_a
Nonsabras	12	100.0	67	88.2

[a]Nonsignificant difference.
[b]Significant difference ($p < 0.01$).

using it almost exclusively in their daily activities. The three tests of the study were: 1) undistorted and uncompeted sentences, as a control to indicate their perception of the test language, Hebrew; 2) speech-masked speech, (+ 3 signal-to-masking ratio), and 3) interrupted speech (10 interruptions per second, with 50% duty cycle).

Table 1 shows that despite equal competence on the control test, the nonsabras were significantly worse than the sabras on the speech-over-babble background, while their scores on the interrupted speech test were not affected significantly. This suggested that the selective listening task was more revealing of the difference in individual linguistic history than the interrupted speech test, which had proved so sensitive to aging.

With these results in hand we undertook a larger study involving 142 subjects, according to the following design:

1. Four populations:
   a. young adult sabras ($N = 25$)
   b. older adult sabras (50–77) ($N = 44$)
   c. young adult nonsabras ($N = 25$)
   d. older adult nonsabras (50–76) ($N = 48$)
   Total subjects = 142
2. Three test materials:
   a. undistorted everyday sentences
   b. similar sentences interrupted 10 times per second
   c. similar sentences heard in competition with a babble of 15 voices

Major variables, therefore, were:
1. *age* (young vs. older (20 *Ss* ages 50–60 and 16 *Ss* ages 61–70) adults)
2. *language background* (those for whom the test language, Hebrew, was the native tongue vs. those for whom the first-learned language was not Hebrew)
3. *Temporally disturbed (periodically interrupted) speech vs. speech masked by a babble of other speech*

Figure 9.2A shows that there is no significant decrement for undistorted speech until past the age of 60, although this time the change ap-

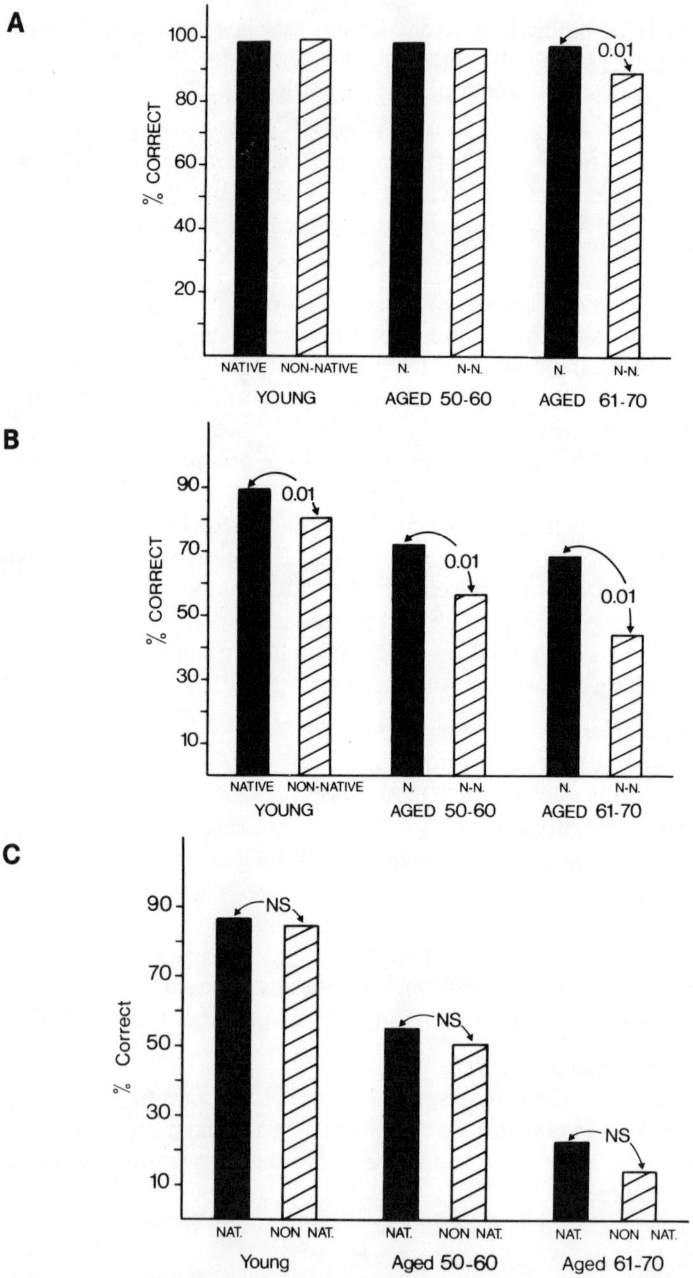

Figure 9.2.   Results on a total of 142 subjects, including young and older adults, native-born talkers of the test language, and non-native–born but fluent talkers of the test language. The different relative scores on the test are discussed in the text. A, Undegraded sentences. B, Against background of other talkers. C, Interrupted speech.

pears only in those who, although fluent in the test language, learned another language as young children.

Figure 9.2B supports the preliminary study made on the young sabras, showing once more the significant disadvantage for non-native listeners, even when young, on the speech-above-babble test, while the interrupted speech test failed to differentiate them from the native-born subjects (Figure 9.2C). These comparative findings are repeated in the older subjects, but with increasing disadvantage, on the selective listening task, for the nonsabras as they grow older. While the aging effect on the interrupted speech test is sharply apparent, this test did not appear to be sensitive to the subjects' linguistic history.

A reexamination of our American data for 60- to 69-year-old Ss from dissimilar backgrounds (native- vs. non-native–born Americans) and on similar tests showed agreement with the Israeli results on the selective listening task but, unlike the Israeli findings, the interrupted speech test did result in a statistically significant difference between the older native and non-native Americans.

Further study is needed to determine whether the consistency of the interrupted speech test in exposing the aging factor is matched by the ability of the selective listening-in-noise test in revealing a persistent deficit in the auditory perception of a second-learned language.

Discussion

It is of interest to explore the probable reasons for the relative breakdown in the perception of a spoken language that was not the first to be mastered in childhood, an observation that has been confirmed recently by Davis, Kastelanski, and Stephens (1976) and Nikam, Beasley, and Rintelmann (1976). What are the apparently critical aspects of receptive language development in the early years of life? Are they related to knowledge of vocabulary or differences in phonemes, in syntactic forms, in prosodic features (if so, which?), or in elaboration through idioms and unique expressions (although the latter was not involved in our studies)? Ellenbogen and Thompson (1972) and Garstecki and Wilkin (1976) suggested that auditory discrimination by speakers of English as a second language may be negatively affected by semantic effects.

An interesting example of the influence of one prosodic feature, rhythm, on speech perception by talkers of various languages was reported by Lotz (1961) as follows: A Czech, a Frenchman, and a Pole listened to three staccato beats, all of equal intensity. When asked about the relative strength of the beats, the Czech reported that the first was the strongest, the Pole selected the middle one as the strongest, and the Frenchman, the final beat. Each subject's decision coincided with the stress pattern in words of his language.

Since the deep structure (the underlying message) of language is relatively universal, it is probable that the details of phonemic patterning (the acoustic characteristics of individual phonemes and the transitions between them), lexicon, prosody, syntax, and semantics, which relate to the surface, or revealing, structure are more strongly implanted in childhood than they can be after the most plastic early period of language learning has passed. The remarkable revelation of findings like ours is the strong effect of this on the *perceptual* processing of speech when the external redundancy of the message has been reduced by degrading the message. This seems to lend support to the so-called active model of speech perception (Stevens and House, 1972), which argues that the listener actively engages his internal set of linguistic rules in order to replicate internally the talker's message. In the context of our interest, it is provocative to note that there is an apparent interaction in which such linguistic limitations in speech perception apparently become even more disturbing with aging.

Dialect Study

Since dialect is a variety of language that may deviate in pronunciation, vocabulary, and grammar from that of the listener, listeners may be expected to experience varying degress of difficulty in understanding talkers speaking unfamiliar dialects. In order to study the differential effects of age on this added complication of speech perception, Susan Kaen, in an unpublished master's thesis at Hunter College in New York City, carried out a revealing study involving young and older adult black and white listeners. She recorded 15 sentences originally constructed by Baratz (1969), which were spoken twice, once by a white, young adult female speaking them in standard English and once by a black young adult female who delivered them in black dialect. For example, one black dialect sentence read "John he always be late for school 'cause he don' like to go to music class." The Standard English equivalent was "John is always late to school because he doesn't like to go to music class." The black nonstandard sentences were designed to reflect the syntax and phonology of the dialect, but not to contain any lexical items that are unique to black dialect. Unfamiliar vocabulary items were therefore not a variable in the study.

The sentences were heard over a babble of a number of talkers, the level of which was 5 dB lower than the sentences. In order to limit the differences between the young and older white subjects, both of the white groups were selected on the basis of their having had very little contact with black dialect. Both older and younger adult black groups were required to have been raised in an environment in which they spoke black

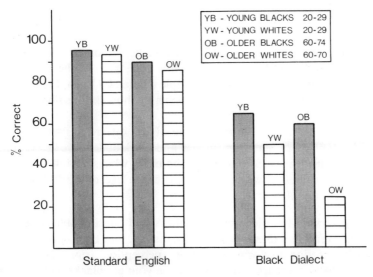

YB - YOUNG BLACKS   20-29
YW - YOUNG WHITES   20-29
OB - OLDER BLACKS   60-74
OW - OLDER WHITES   60-70

Figure 9.3.   Results in a study of speech perception of Standard English and of nonstandard black dialect by white and black subjects, young and older, in age decades as shown.

dialect or were highly exposed to it. Because of the realities of life in the United States, both groups of black subjects had been exposed almost daily to Standard English.

Discussion

The main findings of the study are (see also Figure 9.3):

1. As expected, the black subjects were significantly better than the white subjects in their understanding of the black dialect.
2. The black subjects understood the Standard English significantly better than the white subjects understood the black dialect. (Their scores were three times higher.)
3. As in all other studies reported in this book, the young adult white subjects were significantly better than the older whites in understanding both the black dialect and the Standard English.
4. The young adult blacks were significantly better than the older blacks on the Standard English, but only slightly (nonsignificantly) better on the black dialect. (Many of the older black subjects had been brought up in the South, and black dialect was therefore their first "language.")
5. A surprising finding was that the older blacks were significantly better than the older whites in their understanding of the *Standard English* sentences, while the younger blacks were almost significantly

better than the young whites on the Standard English. In Chapter 3, it was seen that black adults of various ages and work experience showed superior retention of hearing at the audiometric frequencies of 4000 and 8000 Hz than their white colleagues at the same work (ship teamsters). In the limited sample studied by Kaen, the possibility arises that the perception of speech may show similar ethnic differences.

6. When we examined the magnitude of the differences between the understanding of Standard English and black dialect, we saw that the relative drop in performance by the older whites was 40% greater than by the younger whites. The significance level of the differences is smaller than 0.0001.

Even though the older black subjects had considerable experience with the less familiar (Standard English) dialect, they turned in a very significantly inferior performance in its perception (significance level beyond 0.0005) compared with that of the younger blacks, even though there was no significant difference in the perception by these two groups of black dialect. This again illustrates the very much greater difficulty that older adults have than younger adults in understanding a dialect other than their own.

THE ROLE OF MEMORY

Memory as a factor cannot be discussed until we decide what we mean by it. Of the abundance of writings on the subject we shall try to address our interest to that activity in time that seems to enhance or interfere with the understanding of a spoken message. For obvious reasons we shall think of the message as contained primarily in sentences, either spoken in their entirety or implied but only partially expressed. With this imposed limitation we may ask what aspects of perception-memory-recall show age-associated changes related to time factors in the course of listening to the message and processing it for meaning.

The first step in the perception of a spoken message is the reception and momentary storage of auditory units, such as the phonemes and prosodic features. This is probably followed by the short-term storage of combinations of these in terms of syllables, words, and clauses of sentences, but it appears that this does not occur independently, since it is as much a result as a cause of syntactic and semantic mediation. To one who is trying to learn a new language, it is painfully apparent that until such mediation is developed through sufficiently repeated experiences, the spoken message remains a string of meaningless sounds with little memory or recall occurring. Thus it appears that the retention of meaningful chunks of the message can occur only when there is pattern recognition, which in turn depends upon previously stored information. It is clear that the understanding of a spoken message is a complex process critically dependent upon recall of previously stored rules and patterns.

The published literature reports that the immediate repetition, by an older listener, of a string of spoken numbers or letters, often referred to as a test of auditory memory span, yields results not different from those of younger subjects (Bromley, 1958; Gilbert, 1941). Such ritualistic repetition of letters or numbers immediately after exposure does not, however, imply understanding, as witness the peculiar phenomenon of the "parrot speech" of seriously language-disturbed children. When the memory tests of older adults involve storage of some items while others are being repeated aloud, the memory deficits that exist are quickly exposed, as shown previously in reference to the dichotic listening studies on older vs. younger *Ss* (Inglis and Tansey, 1967). Similar evidence emerged from our studies of the role of syntax and semantics in aging speech perception, in which part of a complex or compound sentence must be held in storage while the main idea is registered. Our findings on the disadvantage to the older listener when spoken sentences are long further implicates memory defects.

Finally, it appears from our results, reported in Chapter 8, and from that of others that the semantics (i.e., the implied meanings) are more important than the syntax (e.g., active vs. passive forms) in the memory processes that change with aging (Sach, 1967).

AMOUNT OF AUDIBILITY
REQUIRED FOR COMFORTABLE LISTENING

Amount of audibility required for comfortable listening is concerned with how much intensity above basic threshold a listener requires in order to just comfortably understand a message. A way of testing this is to determine a listener's absolute threshold of awareness of the presence of speech that is still too weak for any discrimination of its sounds or words (this is known as the speech detection threshold, SDT), then to raise the level of the speech until he just barely enjoys intelligibility (the speech reception threshold, SRT). In 20 young listeners, ages 20–30, we found this difference between SDT and SRT to average 8.05 dB. In 17 *Ss* ages 60–70, however, the average required difference was 11.6 dB, which was significantly greater ($p < 0.01$) than for the younger *Ss*. Even more meaningful in noting individual differences, the ranges, within 1 standard deviation, for each group were 5.8 to 10.4 dB for the younger *Ss* and 6.2 to 16.9 dB for the older. It can be expected, therefore, that older persons may require an additional 7 dB or more above their thresholds than younger listeners before they can understand a spoken message. The mean difference for young adults (8.05 dB) in the Hebrew language compares with that of American studies (Chaiklin, 1959; Hirsh et al., 1952), where the differences were reported as 10 (Hirsh et al.) and 9 (Chaiklin) dB, although our mean value for the derived threshold of intelligibility was about 2 dB higher in sound pressure level than in the English-language studies. As in other studies, the range of performance in older subjects is clearly larger than the variations among younger persons.

Another approach to the relative loudness required by older vs. younger persons in order to hear speech acceptably is to ask the subject to indicate the level of the signal he desires for just comfortable understanding when he must listen to it in the presence of competing talkers. We tested 25 young adults (ages 21–27) and 17 60- to 70-year-old subjects, presenting them with a relatively strong background of babble over which they indicated the optimum level for hearing the prime speech signal (a newscast). The older Ss requested an average of 9 dB more signal-to-babble intensity ratio than the young. This coincides closely with the results just cited on the increased sensation level above speech detection required for older listeners to *understand* the speech. In a study we conducted some years ago on blind persons in need of hearing aids, the desired speech-to-babble ratio monaurally was of the same order: 9 dB more than when they listened binaurally. A question that may be raised is: Are the older listeners experiencing less binaural figure-ground separation than younger adults under conditions of competing signals? There are, of course, other possible explanations, related to the tendency of older persons to require more reassurance before responding on a test (Rabbitt, 1968). We have mentioned previously that when tested with a closed set of alternatives in which all possible choices were seen by the testee, older Ss tended to withhold their responses when they were unsure.

EXPERIENCE IN THE LANGUAGE OR DIALECT OF THE TALKER

A common linguistic system between talker and listener is important for the latter's efficient understanding. Even when there are clear differences in their versions of the language being used in their communication, however, a certain measure of successful perception of the message is possible. But as our studies, reported in the section on Effects of the Listener's Language and Dialect History, reveal, the combination of dissimilarity of language background or dialect between the communicants plus degradation of the message by distortion or noise competition results in a significant disturbance of the listener's understanding. This, of course, is a statistical statement, indicating a trend. The extent of this effect varies so greatly that it is risky to predict it for any one "foreign" listener. It has been my personal observation, as one of many linguistic foreigners of my acquaintance in Israel, that despite an apparent high level of fluency in the local tongue, the introduction of distortion, rapid speech as practiced by teenage talkers, and competing speech and noise noticeably increase the relative difficulty of understanding. In short, the less similar the personal linguistic histories of the talker and the listener, the more acoustic cues that are necessary.

COGNITIVE AUDITORY SKILLS

The ability to effect closure when parts of a message are missing (e.g., because of moments of inaudibility or momentary obliterations by noise masking) and to employ an efficient probability system, as expressed in accurate anticipation, is an obvious variable among listeners. Workers in the area of speech perception in children have developed promising test materials and techniques for assessing such abilities, among other auditory skills, in apparently normal as well as learning-troubled school age youngsters (Falck, 1973; Witkin, 1969; Wood, 1971). The evaluation of such auditory abilities has not yet become a part of the test batteries for adults in the audiology centers, although tentative approaches are beginning to be seen, as discussed in Chapter 8. If we are to understand aging speech perception in detail, however, it is incumbent upon us to note not only the tendencies for age-related changes in such auditory skills but also the reasons why some older persons have little or no noticeable difficulty in degraded speech listening while others are seriously affected. This is at least partly because of individual factors like the following.

MOTIVATION, CONFIDENCE, AND THE EFFECTS OF SUGGESTION

Some years ago an illuminating article on motivation was published by Eysenck (1963) in which the concept of conditioned inhibition was presented. In brief, it suggested that as experience of relatively low performance in a task is accumulated, a "negative habit" builds that depresses performance. While such a thesis probably does not enjoy unanimous agreement among psychologists, it is included here as a useful concept.

It would be interesting to note whether such negative habit is a factor in the reduced performance of older persons in their speech performance under difficult listening conditions. That is, do we develop an increasing expectation of relative failure, which leads to reduced performance because of "conditioned inhibition"? A familiar example is that of talking on the telephone when there is disturbance in the room. Older persons are more apt to anticipate and experience failure under such conditions than are younger persons. We have not yet studied the role of conditioned inhibition in aging speech perception, but we have conducted a preliminary study in which we sought to manipulate drive by verbal instructions (suggestion) to young vs. older Ss. We presented three lists of monosyllabic words (modified rhyme test) over a competing babble background to 20 young adults (ages 20–29, mean age 24) and 20 older adults (ages 54–64, mean age 59). One list was given as a control, without suggestion by the examiner. The other two lists were alternately designated by the examiner easy or difficult, from subject to subject, in order to balance out any actual differences between them. In a previous similar study only on young subjects we had learned that three types of responses are generally elicited through such suggestion. Some Ss accept the examiner's characterizations and perform accordingly—better on the easy and worse on the difficult list. Others are apparently influenced in the opposite direction, putting more effort into the difficult list and scoring higher on it. Then there are those who are seemingly uninfluenced by the examiner's descriptions, scoring about equally on the two lists. Our criterion for positive results, that is, signs of some influence of suggestion, was therefore any significant difference in the scores on the easy vs. the difficult lists however way each subject reacted. Of the 20 Ss in each of our study groups, young vs. old, there were 4 young (20%) and 8 older (40%) who showed at least 6% difference in performance on the two lists. The differences ran as high as 32%. When we examined the results of each group for the significance of any and all differences in their subjects' scores on the two lists, we found that the differences were significant for both young and older subjects, but the latter showed very much greater difference ($p < 0.02$ for the young Ss and $p < 0.0001$ for the older Ss). Comparing the magnitudes of the differences between the two groups, we note that the older Ss showed significantly greater effect of the suggestion ($p < 0.001$). Although the samples were small, it is interesting to note a greater tendency by the older subjects to perform better on the list designated difficult than on the easy one. It would be premature to try to analyze the rationale of this early trend. The study does suggest, however, that older persons may be more susceptible to suggestion in their understanding of speech heard over noise.

Self-confidence

It has often been noted in the literature on aging that older persons "tend to be rigid in response to stimuli . . . and adhere unduly to initial impressions" (Smith and Sethi, 1975) and also that they are more cautious than younger adults, tending to withhold a response, in experimental tasks, rather than risk error (Craik, 1962; Silverman, 1963).

In some of our studies both of these tendencies emerged, as reported elsewhere in this book. Such factors as relative caution, rigidity, and defensiveness of a first perception therefore constitute another individual variable in the aging listener.

Stability of Motivation

We are concerned with the consistency of auditory performance under less-than-optimum listening conditions. Audiologists who test the hearing for speech of older persons suffering from presbycusis frequently notice that their discrimination scores may vary dramatically from one test session to another. Thus a patient whose speech discrimination scores range from 72% to 80% at one test session will startle the examiner by scoring 56% to 62% under similar test conditions 1 or 2 weeks later. Is the understanding of speech under certain conditions more unpredictable for older listeners than for younger persons from one communicating period to another? This is another area that invites study in the future. It is suggested, however, that there may be dissimilar findings on a general population of aging persons and patients at audiology and other clinics, since the latter are already troubled by physical complaints and may therefore be less consistent under test conditions.

Vigilance

Some years ago a musicologist friend of mine wrote a charming book on how to enjoy music. In a flashing insight into audition in general he wrote: "For listening to be most productive, it must be *attentive* listening. If we merely let our minds wander, the music will become nothing more than a background to our reveries" (Randolph, 1964). It occurred to me as I recently reread this book that his dictum is applicable to listening to speech as well, and that one of the frequently observed traits of older listeners is a reduced sustained attentiveness. The ability both to remain alert to the occurrence of a message and to continue to listen to it with understanding are referred to as vigilance.

Early vigilance studies by Broadbent (1952, 1953), Mackworth (1948, 1957), and others were concerned with why individuals failed to notice and act upon a signal they were quite able to detect. Continuous experimental attention to this problem explored the effects of prolonged monitoring, and various devices and stratagems were tried for increasing the state of vigilance. These included drugs, reinforcing feedback, rest periods, and the introduction of a new stimulus between exposure to the target (test) stimulus. Thompson, Opton, and Cohen (1963) reported that their studies pointed to speed of presentation as the critical variable, that is, the shorter the time interval between stimuli, the poorer the relative performance of their older Ss. Since the task in their study required perceptual-motor responses, however (a key had to be pushed quickly by the *Ss* at the appearance of the target stimulus), vigilance may not have been the only variable. On a visual task, Surwillo and Quilter (1964) reported that impressive age differences occurred after a prolonged monitoring period (45 min) of a 1-hr test.

While we have not developed recent data on the vigilance aspects of aging speech perception, it is probable that some older persons do not "track" shifts in the content of speech well and there are some for whom continuous speech is, like music for some, "nothing but a background for (their) reveries."

CHAPTER 10

INTERSUBJECT VARIATIONS
IN AGING SPEECH PERCEPTION

One key to understanding aging and particularly to taking action that might extend the human life span can be found in the differences in the rate of aging observed in different individuals.

Nathan W. Shock (1962)

It would be satisfying if, as a result of the many studies of aging speech perception, we could predict the changes and anticipate the decrement in performance at specified age periods. If older persons responded as homogeneously as did young adults on many degraded speech tasks, such prediction might be quite accurate. But a hallmark of findings in studies of aging is the growth in the spread of performance among increasingly older groups of subjects, so that in the 60s, for example, there are those who perform almost as well as young adults and others who exhibit very marked deterioration. It is useful, therefore, to note not only average performance for subjects making up various age groups but also the variations in each group. This provides certain additional benefits as well. If, for example, we find that the scores on a particular test indicate a high degree of uniformity, in a group such as young adults, there is little new information to be gained by testing larger samples of the same group. Conversely, when the variation among scores is relatively large, we get considerably more information as we increase the population sampled (Miller, 1956).

The size of the spread in scores, indicated statistically by the standard deviations about the mean, is related to a combination of the difficulty of the test employed and the ages of the subjects. This is illustrated in Figure 10.1, in which there is a different standard deviation for each test, for both young and older *Ss,* and the easiest test (highest average test score) shows the smallest variances in both groups of subjects. The differences between younger and older subjects are seen clearly in the tendency for the older listeners to diverge from each other markedly (larger standard deviations) as the test becomes more difficult (lowered test scores).

The great increase in the variances with age, on some tasks, suggests that there are middle-age and older persons whose performances on

137

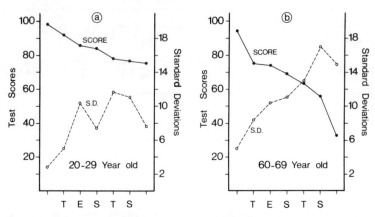

Figure 10.1.   Relationship between standard deviation and difficulty of test, as evidenced by the test scores, in young adults (a) ($N = 36$) and older adults (b) ($N = 41$).

speech perception tasks are especially good or poor compared with the average for their age. It was not unusual, for example, for us to be startled by the near-perfect performance of a 68-year-old woman on the interrupted speech test when each interruption contained speech only 30% of the time followed by silence for the remaining 70% of the time, while many subjects in their early 60s or younger scored 0% on the same test. Such cases illustrate the importance of interpreting individuals separately from statistical group data.

Overlap of results for different age groups has long been noted by gerontologists. Miles (1942) wrote sweepingly: "The range at every adult age of every kind of performance measure is far wider than the difference between means of the most and the least effective age periods of adult life."

The reduction of overlap between groups of different ages depends also upon the difficulty of the test (Figure 10.2). The more difficult test, interrupted speech, resulted in clear separation of the curves for young and older Ss (Figure 10.2a) and the easier speeded speech test (Figure 10.2b) yielded closely overlapping scores, with about 25% of the older Ss scoring higher than the poorest 25% of the younger Ss. The simpler test, therefore, shows considerably fewer age-related differences. Note that the interrupted speech test, which was obviously very difficult for the older subjects, still permitted a high degree of homogeneity of performance among the young adults. Plotting the distribution of scores within each group in this manner makes it clear that the interrupted speech test is uniquely sensitive to aging.

Another illustration of the differences in variances and absence of overlap, revealed by a test of the effects of levels of probability (see

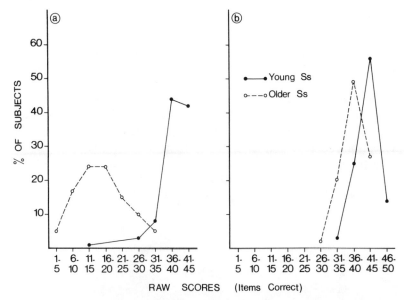

RAW   SCORES   (Items Correct)

Figure 10.2.   Percentage of subjects achieving various scores on a difficult test (a)—inter-rupted speech—and on an easier test (b)—speeded speech. The more difficult test more clearly separates the older subjects' performances from those of the younger subjects.

Chapter 8), is shown in Figure 10.3, in which the score of *each* subject is shown, with each curve beginning at the left with the lowest score in the group and proceeding systematically toward the highest score. The shallowness of the curve and the resultant small standard deviation for the young *Ss* contrast sharply with the greater variation in the older group of

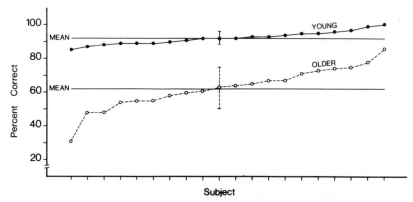

Figure 10.3.   Plots of scores on each subject of two groups (young and older adults) obtained on a test of speech perception, showing a virtual lack of overlap of performances between them, as well as the greater tendency of the scores of one group (young) toward homogeneity among its subjects. The resultant standard deviation about each mean is shown vertically in the center.

Ss. Plotting the results of the two groups to be compared in this manner has the added feature that near-total separation of scores—where there is overlap of only one score of each group—stands out clearly. Such a test can thus be seen to distinguish the behavior of groups for almost all of their members.

It is not to be expected that all tests of auditory perception will show such clear differences in individual as well as group scores, but the one general principle that is supported repeatedly in studies of aging speech perception is that the harder the task, the greater the variance in the older subjects. Whether there is once again a convergence of performance within the age group in the final decline of the most advanced years has not yet been tested by us or, apparently, reported by others.

CHAPTER 11

CROSS-SECTIONAL VS. LONGITUDINAL STUDIES

CONTENTS

Earlier we discussed some of the advantages and disadvantages of horizontal, or cross-sectional, sampling, in which each group of subjects represents a different age period, such as decades, and of longitudinal studies, in which some subjects are retested periodically as they grow older. In all aspects of hearing, however, while there have been numerous reports based upon cross-sectional samplings, there is a notable lack in the literature on longitudinal hearing studies. An exception was a recent report of a longitudinal study of presbycusis among men in their 60s ($N=71$) and others between 70 and 90 years of age ($N=42$) (Milne, 1977). Milne found no discernible change in either age group after 1 year, but after 5 years the increase in presbycusic hearing loss was clear, with the shift in audiograms even more pronounced in the 70- to 90-year-old men than in those in their 60s (Figure 11.1).

In what appears to have been the only longitudinal study of aging speech perception so far, we conducted two follow-ups on samples of subjects we had first tested in 1966 and 1967. The elapsed time averaged 3 years at the first follow-up and 7 years and 8½ months at the second.

THE 3-YEAR FOLLOW-UP

The 3-year follow-up study involved 54 of the original 282 Ss and included 15 who were ages 40–49 at the time of the first study, 14 ages 50–59, 12 ages 60–69, and 13 ages 70–79. The same test battery, equipment, test recordings, and procedures of the earlier study were employed. Although 11 of these 54 Ss had a first language other than English and in general scored lower than the native-born American Ss of their age groups, there was no consistent pattern of change that suggested a difference in the rate of

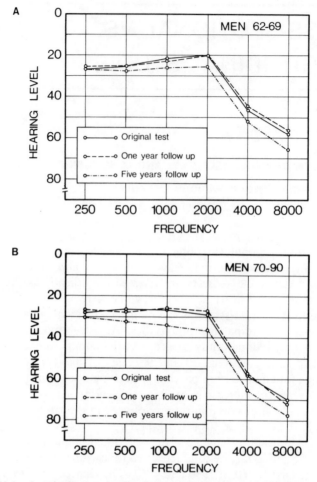

Figure 11.1.   Longitudinal study of audiometric thresholds of aging men of two age groups in Edinburgh, Scotland. (From J. S. Milne, *British Journal of Audiology 11* (1), pp. 7–14, 1977, with permission.)

decrement. The data for both native and non-native talkers of English were therefore consolidated for Figure 11.2a. The figure illustrates that even in a period of 3 years, while there is no noticeable change in the hearing for undegraded speech, the perception of degraded speech undergoes decrement in persons who are over 60 years old.

THE 7-YEAR FOLLOW-UP

Four years after the first follow-up study, 55 of the original 282 *Ss* were retested, having aged an average of 7 years and 8½ months since their

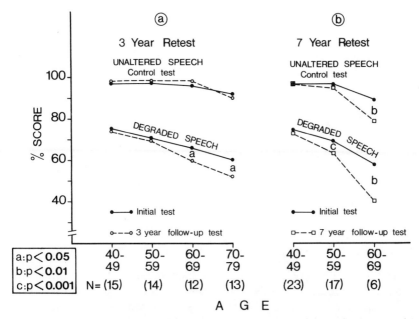

Figure 11.2.   Longitudinal study of perception of degraded speech by 54 *Ss* (3-year study) and 55 *Ss* (7-year study). Significances of the changes are shown. The average results on subjects age 40 or over only are shown, accounting for the lower total *N* in the figure for the 7-year retest.

first tests. Although these 55 included 19 who had also been retested in the 3-year follow-up, the later study included younger subjects than in the earlier follow-up, beginning with some who were originally in the 20–29 age decade and sampling some in each successive decade up to 60–69. The latter were now mostly in their 70s.

Results

There was no significant change (Figure 11.2b) in the performance of *Ss* from 20 through 59 years of age on the control test, in which the test sentences were heard under optimum conditions, without distortion or competing noises or speech. In the 60–69 age decade, however, there was a significant deterioration ($p < 0.01$), even on this control test. These results, shown in Figure 11.2b, agree with our earlier horizontally sampled findings using lists of simple words (Blumenfeld et al., 1969) and those of Pestalozza and Shore (1955).

In the degraded speech tests, a significant decrement ($p < 0.001$) occurs first in the 50- to 59-year-old *Ss,* followed by an even greater average drop in the 60- to 69-year-old *Ss.* These decrements are clearly larger than those seen after 3 years, apparently documenting further the continuous changes taking place from age 60 on.

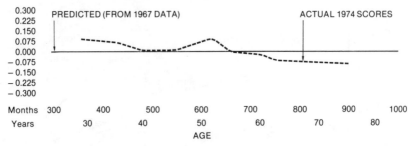

Figure 11.3. Composite residuals (deviations) of actual 1974 scores from scores predicted for each age, in months, from the 1967 study. The 1967 scores were cross-sectional on a population of 185 subjects. The 1974 scores are for 53 of these subjects retested after an average of 7.7 years, located according to their ages at the most recent test. (Ordinate altered by arc sin transformation Y = 2 arc sin√Proportion.) (From M. Bergman et al., *Journal of Gerontology 31,* p. 537, 1976, with permission.)

COMPARISON OF CROSS-SECTIONAL AND LONGITUDINAL RESULTS

In order to compare the results obtained by these two sampling approaches, we derived a predicted score for each subject of the 7-year follow-up study based upon the data of subjects whose ages in months at the time of the original cross-sectional study were the same as the ages in months that our subjects had reached by the time of the follow-up. Thus we could compare the difference between their younger performance and that of the then-older subjects (a cross-sectional comparison) with the difference between their original scores and their later performances (giving longitudinal data). Because of the presence of inconsistent statistical-difference criteria in percentage scores, the data were converted by arc sine transform (Brownlee, 1965) for plotting on Figure 11.3, which shows the relationship between such predicted aging scores and the actual scores obtained by the follow-up testing. It is interesting to note that whereas the younger *Ss* tended to perform slightly better, the older *Ss* tended to do worse than predicted. In general, however, it seems reasonable to conclude that in these admittedly limited studies, the cross-sectional and longitudinal approaches yielded similar results, which provide additional support for our main findings of age-related decline.

RELATIVE AGING AMONG VARIOUS LISTENING TASKS

The longitudinal data for the 55 *Ss* afford us an opportunity to note whether the aging effect is relatively equal from one listening task to another. That is, if a subject performed better on one task than on another in the original study, would he show the same relative performances years later? We studied this by comparing the ranking of scores for each

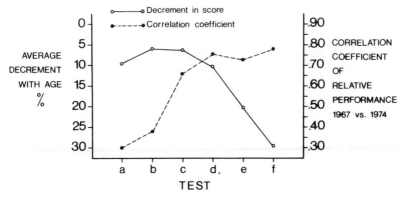

Figure 11.4. Consistency (correlation coefficient) of relative rank of scores obtained on six different tests on subjects tested in 1967 and again in 1974, compared with the amount of decrement of the actual scores during the same period. See text for calculation of details.

subject in his first performance with the ranking of his scores on the same tests obtained on the 7-year follow-up study. The results yielded correlation coefficients ranging from 0.30 for one listening task to 0.78 for another, all of which were statistically significant. Considering the range of correlations, however, it was tempting to see whether the relative consistency of aging changes revealed by each task was related to its difficulty (that is, its scores at the original test). Figure 11.4 was constructed partly from the original, cross-sectional study by calculating the average decrease in scores for each older age decade from the scores of the 20- to 29-year-old *Ss*. These decrements of each of the four decades were added, and the sum was divided by 4, yielding the *average decrement* over the decades 30–39 through 60–69. This was done for the scores of each listening task. The average decrement for each was then plotted against the correlation coefficient of the 1967 vs. 1974 scores for each test.

Interpretation

The tests that showed the most decrement with age in our first, cross-sectional studies showed the highest correlations in relative decrement in the longitudinal study, and vice versa. This indicates once again that the more sensitive (i.e., more discriminating) tests for aging speech perception will more accurately indicate the relative changes an individual will suffer as he continues to grow older. Put another way, those tasks that result in only small differences among *Ss* of different age groups show little consistency, with aging, in the relative performance they evoke, whereas the tasks that expose large decrements in successively older groups of *Ss* tend to produce highly consistent relative performance in subjects followed longitudinally.

CHAPTER 12

SUMMARY AND
CONCLUDING OBSERVATIONS

CONTENTS

RECAPITULATION

Our purpose was to relate the perception of speech to the aging process. We noted, in the first chapter, that a variety of approaches may be pursued in order to illuminate a listener's understanding of spoken messages of various levels of complexity, heard under different conditions of difficulty. Even without undertaking formal studies it is apparent that middle-age and older persons who are not considered to be hearing impaired "hear" speech apparently well under easy listening conditions. Were we interested only in the "best" performance that can be observed when the message is simple and the listening conditions highly favorable, as in a one-to-one conversation in a quiet room, we would be content to conclude that only a noticeable loss of hearing interferes with audition as one ages and that the decrement in auditory performance in such cases can be adequately described on the basis of the degree and type of hearing impairment. It has been the burden of this book, however, to stress that the understanding of speech in daily life undergoes gradual change, with increasing age, because of a combination of peripheral and central alterations, even in the absence of a significant hearing loss, and that such alterations significantly affect the understanding of speech that is heard under less-than-optimal conditions.

In Chapter 2 it was seen that sensory perceptions other than auditory also undergo changes with age, and that much research effort has been invested in vision, with results that bear considerable likeness to those we are obtaining in audition. Particularly striking is the close parallel between the findings in vision and audition when the task involves central restructuring of a verbal message from which portions have been deleted.

When we turned our attention to the phenomenon of presbycusis we noted that published curves of aging hearing sensitivity vary greatly, mostly because of the differences in the population sampled by the researchers. We presented preliminary findings that suggest age-related alterations in function of the peripheral hearing mechanism even before audiometric changes become evident, and offered this as emerging evidence of at least partial complicity of the peripheral system in the demonstrable decrement in the understanding of degraded speech as early as 50 years of age.

Chapter 4 presented support for the inference that the decline in speech perception with advancing age is related in large part to changes in the central nervous system.

Chapter 5 introduced the field studies that followed by detailing the experimental decisions that need to be made when designing such studies of aging speech perception, for example, which populations to sample and which test materials to use. A central point is the inappropriateness of using clinical lists of test words as a measure for this purpose. Included also is the argument that only through the use of materials and test conditions that stress the auditory system will different aspects of age-related decline be exposed, and a list of suggested methods is provided for degrading the speech signals used for such studies.

After a brief introduction (Chapter 6) to the studies we have carried out over the past 14 years, Chapter 7 presents our results when the physical aspects of the message were manipulated to provide different degrees of signal degradation. Variables that were employed included: 1) *time* (altering the amount of exposure to the signal, which was periodically interrupted, and speeding and slowing the spoken message), 2) *frequency* (low-pass and band-pass filtering were used), 3) *masking* (electronically generated noise, speech babble, and intelligible "perceptual" masking were included), 4) *reverberation* (i.e., the acoustics of the listening environment), 5) *transmission characteristics* (the telephone and the hearing aid served as experimental transmission conditions), and 6) *talker differences*.

From the results of the foregoing it was deduced that, given brief exposures to a speech signal, middle-age and older listeners will perceive only a fraction as much as the younger listener and will benefit less from small increases in the exposure time. Speeding the message either by talking faster or by electronically compressing it was seen to penalize the older listener, whether his required response was a spoken repetition of the test message or a motor act, as in the token test. The latter test suggested that age-related decrement in the understanding of spoken instructions probably involves codification, organization, and storage.

Filtering out the higher frequencies of speech, in apparent combination with presbycusic changes in the peripheral auditory system, revealed greater reliance by older listeners than in younger adults on information embedded in the frequencies above 2000 Hz. This is of special importance in the interpretation of noise-induced hearing loss, which generally reaches disturbing levels in middle and later age after years of exposure.

Our studies were consistent with those of others in revealing a failure of selective listening as an age-accompanied problem in the hearing of speech in the presence of competing auditory signals. An additional finding was that short bursts of noise, which are more disturbing to the perception of speech than are short periods of silent interruption, caused a disproportionately greater problem in aging than in younger adults.

We found that the concept of acceptability of room acoustics (revealed most directly through the measurement of its reverberation time) must be corrected for age. What is only a mildly unfavorable reverberation time for young adults results in progressively greater breakdown in speech understanding with advancing age. The effect is apparently as though the reverberation (i.e., decay) time were made increasingly more unfavorable.

Our tests through the telephone system provided support for the frequent complaint by older adults of difficulties in its use, particularly when there is competing noise in the listening room. It was suggested that consideration should be given to the introduction of binaural listening, as well as to improvement of the telephone's characteristics.

Listening to speech through a monaural hearing aid was seen to impose significant limitations, both in younger and older adults, but once again the penalty extracted from the older listener is significantly larger. This is a distressing situation in view of the fact that by far the largest proportion of hearing aid users is drawn from that group, which also suffers the additional burden imposed upon the understanding of speech by the complications of sensorineural hearing impairment. The disruption of speech perception is even greater when the aided hearing must serve for a variety of talkers, each of whose characteristics of voice, articulation, and prosodic features interact with the characteristics of the hearing aid differently. Our several studies on the differential effects of such talker characteristics resulted in findings that under a severe condition of degradation (periodic interruption), as well as when there is no distortion in or competition with the speech signal, the disturbance of understanding of different talkers in older adults is significantly greater and more varied than in younger listeners, with whispered speech causing particular frustrations for aging listeners.

In Chapter 8 we turned from the effects of the physical aspects of the speech signal to its linguistics. We found that the compound sentence, when heard in the presence of a babble of other talkers, resulted in significantly poorer understanding for older listeners than the simple or complex sentence form. This effect was exacerbated even more when the test material was not the older subject's first-learned language.

A corollary study, in which the subordinate clause of complex sentences was either of the right-branching construction or was centrally embedded in the sentence, revealed, in common with the previous study, that memory plays an important role in the aging decline of understanding of complex and compound sentences.

The influence of the semantics of a message was investigated in studies in which the range of alternative possible words and the level of a word's probability of occurrence (that is, of its inference from the remainder of a sentence) were manipulated. The increasing redundancy that should accompany a smaller number of possible words provided significantly less benefit for the older Ss than for younger adults. Similarly, when the same test words were presented twice, once without contextual clues and once with such clues, or "pointers," in the remainder of the sentence, the older Ss failed to utilize the advantages of the contextual information as well as the younger Ss.

In the next chapter we looked at various factors in the listener that contribute to his relative age-related success or failure in the understanding of degraded speech. We presented findings from a number of studies on the effects of a listener's language or dialect history on his understanding of degraded speech, supporting still further the theory that if the language or dialect to which he is listening is different from what he first learned as a young child, he will probably never overcome the disadvantage this imposes.

In the same chapter we saw that older listeners require more intensity above their threshold of hearing and above noise in order to understand speech comfortably and that they tend to be more suggestible regarding the amount of difficulty to be expected in a difficult listening situation.

Among the most compellingly consistent results of our studies, as well as of those reported in other investigations of aging behavior, is the increasing variability of performance among listeners of the same age. This variability is related, in turn, to the difficulty of the task, the more demanding tests resulting in a greater spread of scores among the older subjects.

Finally we looked at the relationship between the findings of longitudinal vs. cross-sectional studies of aging speech perception and found, in the only study that seems to have included both sampling techniques on this topic, that there was little difference in the information yielded, since both approaches were closely consistent in revealing the same age-related decrements. An important statistic that emerges from our longitudinal studies is that for a difficult listening task there is high probability that a person who does relatively well on it at an earlier period in his advancing years will repeat his relatively good performance in later years, and vice versa.

DISCUSSION

The results of our studies and those of others share a basic weakness. We depend upon a *response* from the subject as evidence of how a signal was perceived. One way to reveal the influence of this is to vary the mode of response, as we did when we required motor responses on the token test in place of spoken responses by the subjects. This, however, still leaves factors related to more general age-related effects, such as the increasing *caution* of older adults in their commitment to a response. As Schaie (1975, pp. 122–123) observed, "Young people in most test situations tend to make many more errors of commission than omission, but the reverse is true for the elderly." This, he concluded, "may make the elderly appear less able than they actually are."

It is clear that our studies and others reported here and elsewhere are but a small beginning, because to discuss aging and the perception of speech is to imply a multitude of auditory abilities and behaviors. These are essentially situational and therefore appear differently at different times. We have not yet arrived at a single summary index, like the IQ statistic for intelligence, or a descriptive profile to illuminate the relative successes and failures of an individual on the highly variegated auditory demands made upon him. Without addressing the desirability of summary information in such forms, it is apparent that we must expose those situations and conditions of listening in which the auditory behavior of middle-age and older persons deviates noticeably from that of younger listeners.

A promising lead in the understanding of age-related changes in speech perception, as in other aspects of aging behavior, is probably to be found in the fact that as we age we are increasingly more unlike each other than when we are young adults. Studies like ours repeatedly find that where one subject of a given advanced age may score close to or as well as young adults, others show near-catastrophic breakdown on a demanding perceptual task. This suggests that in-depth analyses of such contrasting behavior may reveal associated factors. Since the integrating role of the central nervous system seems to be critically involved in this declining behavior, as in other functional aspects of aging, such analyses would be expected to draw heavily upon the knowledge and procedures developed in the field of gerontology.

A provocative question that arises concerns the relationship between the relative decline in the understanding of degraded speech and an aging individual's opportunity for continued exercise of the skills of speech perception. Miles (1942, p. 765) reported that in motor activity (promptness of hand response), 65% of 50- to 69-year old *Ss* exceeded the performance of 18- to 49-year-olds. He suggested that it is possible that "the habit of continued use in the hand response may play no small part in the total picture." In our longitudinal studies we found that the superior performers on our most difficult tests remained superior 8 years later. It would be illuminating to know whether they "exercised" these auditory skills more in the intervening years than their less effective cohorts.

WHAT CAN WE DO ABOUT IT?

There seem to be two approaches to the amelioration of the undesirable effects of the decline in speech perception skills with age. We can try to affect the degenerative biological influences in the individual and we can change some of the conditions of spoken communication to accommodate them to the changes in the aging listener. The latter appears to be more immediately accessible to decision-making and action. Control of the acoustics of listening environments, particularly public areas like churches and meeting halls, should not pose serious problems, if the interest exists. Similarly, communication equipment, such as the telephone, public address systems, and radio and television design should be reexamined in light of the emerging knowledge of the limitations inherent in the increased life-span of such a growing proportion of our population. An obvious focus for enlightened technology is in the design of the hearing aid, which is now of such dubious value to so many aging, hearing-impaired persons. It is apparent also that the increases in the ongoing noise levels in our society could be controlled, given sufficient public interest, to reduce the number of daily situations in which the aging listener must exercise his tenuous selective listening abilities. In short, the time has arrived for the development of a corps of specialists who will continue to expose the communication limitations and resultant needs of middle-age and older persons and who can advise on the required corrective measures.

On the approach to the biological realities of aging there is a growing body of professional workers who are devoting major efforts to all aspects of behavior, including those involved in perception. Auditory perception, particularly for speech heard under a variety of conditions, has not yet shared significantly in these efforts.

Drug therapy has often been reported and applied as a means for improving the general functioning of aging persons. Woodruff (1975), for example, reported that estrogen replacement gives promise of the maintenance of desired hormone levels. Antonelli (1970) reported on the attempts, in Italy, to influence the perception of degraded speech through the administration of drug therapy. While the results were not definitive, there did appear to be noticeable effects, both positive and negative, from the use of amphetamines and barbiturates, respectively, probably acting upon the reticular system of the brainstem. Another report on the effect of drugs on the perception of speech is that of Thaler, Fass, and Fitzpatrick (1973), who stated that during a marijuana high, volunteer subjects, all with prior experience with marijuana, showed greatly improved speech discrimination for low-intensity speech and for speech heard in a high-noise background.

The possibility that continued exercise of auditory skills, such as listening in noisy environments, may enhance the ability suggests that training might be an approach to the reversal of the decline we have noted. The feasibility of this approach, however, would have to be studied. It is not clear, for example, whether the changes in speech perception under unfavorable conditions can be linked to a reduction in sensory input, since the decline has been observed in our studies to begin in early middle age. It is possible, of course, that the more rapid changes we reported for the 7th decade of life *are* due, in part, to understimulation.

There must certainly be additional perceptual abilities in man as in other animal species. As we emerge slowly from our still-limited understanding, we will undoubtedly recognize significant untapped resources for compensating, reducing, or even negating certain aspects of behavioral decrement. Compelling examples of poorly understood perceptions are seen in the remarkable navigational feats of fish and birds, who often travel thousands of miles for breeding or returning to their natural homes. Similarly, the dim view we now have of our ability to control, through biofeedback, our body functions formerly believed to be entirely automatic may grow to illuminate possible functional approaches to the better control of stress, which apparently plays a detrimental role in the understanding of degraded speech by older persons.

The world is now teeming with people who have reached middle age or beyond, and with the increasing interest in zero population growth the proportion of such adults will continue to rise. Whereas in early times there was little incentive to worry about behavioral decline in what we now recognize as the "middle" and later years, we are coming face-to-face with the realities of this rapidly growing and increasingly important stratum of our species. Our penchant for planning education, communication equipment and standards, and other aspects and trappings of social linguistic functioning, as though this were still primarily a youth-populated world, raises new problems for the coming majority when it does not discourage them from participating. It is time to understand these problems and to organize our resources to meet them.

REFERENCES

Abbs, J. H., and H. M. Sussman. 1971. Neurophysiologic feature detectors and speech perception: A discussion of theoretical implications. J. Speech Hear. Res. 14:23-26.

Abel, M. 1972. The visual trace in relation to aging. Unpublished doctoral dissertation, Washington University, St. Louis, Mo.

American National Standards Institute. 1969. Methods for the Calculation of the Articulation Index, ANSI S3.5-1969. American National Standards Institute, New York.

Antonelli, A. R. 1970. Sensitized speech tests in aged people. In C. Rojskjaer (ed.), Speech Audiometry. Second Danavox Symposium, Odense, Denmark.

Atherley, G. R. C., and W. G. Noble. 1971. Clinical picture of occupational hearing loss obtained with the Hearing Measurement Scale. In D. W. Robinson (ed.), Occupational Hearing Loss, p. 203. Academic Press, New York.

Baltes, P. B. 1968. Longitudinal and cross-sectional sequences in the study of age and generation effects. Hum. Dev. 11(3):145-171.

Baratz, J. I. 1969. A bi-dialectical task for determining language proficiency in economically disadvantaged children. Child Dev. 40:889-910.

Beasley, D., B. Forman, and W. Rintelmann. 1972. Perception of time compressed CNC monosyllables by normal listeners. J. Audiol. Res. 12:71-75.

Beasley, D. S., S. Schwimmer, and W. F. Rintelmann. 1972. Intelligibility of time-compressed CNC monosyllables. J. Speech Hear. Res. 15:340-350.

Bergman, M. 1966. Hearing in the Mabaans. Arch. Otolaryngol. 84:411-415.

Bergman, M. 1971. Hearing and aging. Audiology 10:164-171.

Bergman, M., V. Blumenfeld, D. Cascardo, B. Dash, H. Levitt, and M. Margulies. 1976. Age-related decrement in hearing for speech; sampling and longitudinal studies. J. Gerontol. 31:533-538.

Bergman, M., S. Hirsch, and T. Najenson. 1977. Test of auditory perception in the assessment and management of patients with cerebral cranial injury. Scand. J. Rehab. Med. 9:173-177.

Birren, J. E. 1965. Age changes in speed of behavior: Its central nature and physiological correlates. In A. T. Welford and J. E. Birren (eds.), Behavior, Aging and the Nervous System. Charles C Thomas Publisher, Springfield, Ill.

Birren, J. E., and V. Clayton. 1975. History of gerontology. In D. S. Woodruff and J. E. Birren (eds.), Aging: Scientific Perspectives and Social Issues. Van Nostrand Reinhold Co., New York.

Birren, J. E., and K. W. Schaie (eds.). 1977. Handbook of the Psychology of Aging. Van Nostrand Reinhold Co., New York.

Blumenfeld, V. G., M. Bergman, and E. Millner. 1969. Speech discrimination in an aging population. J. Speech Hear. Res. 12:210-217.

Bocca, E., and C. Calearo. 1956. Aspects of auditory pathology of central origin in aged subjects. Ann. Laringol. 55:365-369.

Botwinick, J. 1971. Research problems and concepts in the study of aging. In F. G. Scott and R. M. Brewer (eds.), Perspectives in Aging, I. Research Focus, Oregon Center for Gerontology.

Boyle, E., A. M. Aparicio, J. Kaye, and M. Acker. 1975. Auditory and visual memory losses in aging populations. J. Am. Geriatr. Soc. 23:284-286.

Braunmühl, A. v. 1957. Handbuch der speziellen pathologischen Anatomie und Histologie. [Handbook of Special Pathological Anatomy and Histology.] Lubarsch-Henske-Rossle, Berlin.

Broadbent, D. E. 1952. Failures of attention in selective listening. J. Exp. Psychol. 44:51–55.

Broadbent, D. E. 1953. Classical conditioning and human watch keeping. Psychol. Rev. 60:331–339.

Broadbent, D. E. 1954. The role of auditory localization in attention and memory span. J. Exp. Psychol. 47:191–196.

Brody, H. 1955. Organization of the cerebral cortex. J. Comp. Neurol. 102:511–556.

Bromley, D. B. 1958. Some effects of age on short term learning and remembering. J. Gerontol. 13:398–406.

Brownlee, V. A. 1965. Statistical Theory and Methodology in Science and Engineering. 2nd Ed. John Wiley & Sons, New York.

Bunch, C. C. 1929. Age variations in auditory acuity. AMA Arch. Otolaryngol. 9:625–636.

Bunch, C. C., and T. S. Raiford. 1931. Race and sex variations in auditory acuity. Arch. Otolaryngol. 13:423–434.

Calearo, C., and A. Lazzaroni. 1957. Speech intelligibility in relation to the speed of the message. Laryngoscope 67:410–419.

Carhart, R., and S. Nicholls. 1971. Perceptual masking in elderly persons. Paper presented at the annual meeting of the American Speech and Hearing Association, November, Chicago, Ill.

Chaiklin, J. B. 1959. The relation among three selected auditory speech thresholds. J. Speech Hear. Res. 2:237–242.

Cooper, J. G., and B. P. Cutts. 1971. Speech discrimination in noise. J. Speech Hear. Res. 14:332–337.

Corso, J. F. 1971. Sensory processes and age effects in normal adults. J. Gerontol. 26:90–105.

Craik, F. I. M. 1962. The effects of age and the experimental situation on confidence behaviour. Bull. Br. Psychol. Soc. 47:21 (abstr.).

Craik, F. I. M. 1968. Short-term memory and the aging process. In G. A. Talland (ed.), Human Aging and Behavior. Academic Press, New York.

Craik, F. I. M. 1977. Age differences in human memory. In J. E. Birren and K. W. Schaie (eds.), Handbook of the Psychology of Aging. Van Nostrand Reinhold Co., New York.

Davies, D. R. 1968. Age differences in paced inspection tasks. In G. A. Talland (ed.), Human Aging and Behavior. Academic Press, New York.

Davis, R. J., W. Kastelanski, and S. D. G. Stephens. 1976. Some factors influencing the results of speech tests of central auditory function. Scand. Audiol. 5:179–186.

DeRenzi, E., and L. A. Vignolo. 1962. The token test: A sensitive test to detect receptive disturbances in aphasia. Brain 85:665–678.

Eisdorfer, C. 1968. Arousal and performance: Experiments in verbal learning and a tentative theory. In G. A. Talland (ed.), Human Aging and Behavior. Academic Press, New York.

Eisdorfer, C., S. Axelrod, and F. L. Wilkie. 1963. Stimulus exposure time as a factor in serial learning in an aged sample. J. Abnorm. Psychol. 67:594–600.

Eisdorfer, C., and F. Wilkie. 1972. Auditory changes in the aged: A follow-up study. J. Am. Geriatr. Soc. 20:377–382.

Ellenbogen, E. M., and G. R. Thompson. 1972. A comparison of social class effects in 2 tests of auditory discrimination. J. Learn. Disabil. 5:209–212.

Eysenck, H. J. 1963. The measurement of motivation. Sci. Am. May:130–140.

Falck, V. T. 1973. Auditory processing for the child with language disorders. Except. Child. February:413–416.

Feldman, R., and S. Reger. 1967. Relations among hearing, reaction time and age. J. Speech Hear. Res. 10:479–495.

Fletcher, H. 1953. Speech and Hearing in Communication. Van Nostrand Reinhold Co., New York.

Fodor, J., and M. Garrett. 1967. Some syntactic determinants of sentential complexity. Percept. Psychophys. 2(7).

Fozard, J. L., E. Wolf, B. Bell, R. A. McFarland, and S. Podolsky. 1977. Visual perception and communication. In J. E. Birren and K. W. Schaie (eds.), The Psychology of Aging. Van Nostrand Reinhold Co., New York.

French, N. R., and J. C. Steinberg. 1947. Factors governing the intelligibility of speech sounds. J. Acoust. Soc. Am. 19:90–119.

Gacek, R. R., and H. F. Schuknecht. 1969. Pathology of presbycusis. Int. Audiol. 8(2–3):199–207.

Gaeth, J. 1948. A study of phonemic regression in relation to hearing loss. Doctoral dissertation. Northwestern University, Evanston, Ill.

Garstecki, D. C., and M. K. Wilkin. 1976. Linguistic background and test material considerations in assessing sentence identification ability in English- and Spanish-English-speaking adolescents. J. Am. Audiol. Soc. 6:263–268.

Gilbert, J. G. 1941. Memory loss in senescence. J. Abnorm. Soc. Psychol. 36: 73–86.

Glorig, A., D. Wheeler, M. A. Quiggle, D. Grings, and A. Summerfield. 1957. 1954 Wisconsin State Fair Hearing Survey. Subcommittee on Noise in Audiology. Am. Acad. Ophthalmol. Otolaryngol. 111 pp.

Goetzinger, C. P., G. O. Proud, D. Dirks, and J. Embry. 1961. A study of hearing in advanced age. AMA Arch. Otolaryngol. 73:662–674.

Goetzinger, C., and C. Rousey. 1959. Hearing problems in later life. Med. Times 87:771–780.

Granick, S., and J. E. Birren. 1969. Cognitive functioning of survivors versus non-survivors. Paper presented at the 8th International Congress of Gerontology, Washington, D.C.

Hansen, C. C., and E. Reske-Nielsen. 1965. Pathological studies in presbycusis. Arch. Otolaryngol. 82:115–132.

Harbert, R., I. Young, and H. Menduke. 1966. Audiological findings in presbycusis. J. Aud. Res. 6:297–312.

Harris, J. D. 1965. Auditory perception. Short course presented at the annual meeting of the American Speech and Hearing Association, November.

Herman, G. E., L. R. Warren, and J. W. Wagener. 1977. Auditory lateralization: Age differences in sensitivity to dichotic time and amplitude cues. J. Gerontol. 32:187–191.

Heron, A., and S. Chown. 1967. Age and Function. J. & A. Churchill Ltd., London.

Hinchcliffe, R. 1962. The anatomical locus of presbycusis. J. Speech Hear. Disord. 27:301–310.

Hirsh, I. J. 1967. Perception of speech. In A. B. Graham (ed.), Sensorineural Hearing Processes and Disorders. Little, Brown & Co., Boston.

Hirsh, I. J., H. Davis, S. R. Silverman, E. G. Reynolds, E. Eldert, and R. W. Benson. 1952. Development of materials for speech audiometry. J. Speech Hear. Disord. 17:321–337.

House, A. S., C. E. Williams, H. L. Hecker, and K. D. Kryter. 1965. Articulation-testing methods: Consonantal differentiation with a closed-response set. J. Acoust. Soc. Am. 37:158–166.

Hume, L. E. 1978. The aural-overload test: Twenty years later. J. Speech Hear. Disord. 43:34–46.

Inglis, J., and W. K. Caird. 1963. Age difference in successive responses to simultaneous stimulation. Can. J. Psychol. 17:98–105.

Inglis, J., and C. L. Tansey. 1967. Age differences in dichotic listening performance. J. Psychol. 66:325–332.

International Standards Organization (ISO). 1975. Acoustics—Standard Reference Zero for the Calibration of Pure-Tone Audiometers, ISO 389-1975. International Organization for Standardization, Geneva. (Also available as ANSI S3.6-1969.)

Jatho, K. 1969. Population surveys and norms. Int. Audiol. 8(2–3):231–239.

Jerger, J. 1973. Audiological findings in aging. Adv. Otorhinolaryngol. 20:115–124. Basel.

Johnson, R. C., R. E. Cole, J. K. Bowers, S. V. Foiles, J. W. Patrick, and R. E. Woliver. 1979. Hemisphere efficiency in middle and later adulthood. Cortex 15:109–119.

Kaen, S. 1972. A bi-dialectical comparison of hearing for speech in white vs. black listeners, with age as a variable. Doctoral thesis, Hunter College, New York.

Kalikow, D. N., K. N. Stevens, and L. L. Elliott. 1977. Development of a test of speech intelligibility in noise using sentences with controlled word predictability. J. Acoust. Soc. Am. 61:1337–1351.

Karsai, L. K., M. Bergman, and Y. B. Choo. 1972. Hearing in ethnically different longshoremen. Arch. Otolaryngol. 96:499–504.

Katz, J. 1962. The use of staggered spondaic words for assessing the integrity of the central nervous system. J. Aud. Res. 2:327–337.

Keith, R. W. (ed.). 1977. Central Auditory Dysfunction. Grune & Stratton, New York.

Kimura, D. 1961. Cerebral dominance and the perception of verbal stimuli. Can. J. Psychol. 15:166–171.

Kirikae, I. 1969. Auditory function in advanced age with reference to histological changes in the central auditory system. Int. Audiol. 8(2–3):221–230.

Kirikae, I., T. Sato, and T. Shitara. 1964. Study of hearing in advanced age. Laryngoscope 74:205–220.

Konig, E. 1957. Pitch discrimination and age. Acta Otolaryngol. 48:475–489.

Konigsmark, B. W. 1969a. Neuronal population of the ventral cochlear nucleus in man. Anat. Rec. 163:212–213.

Konigsmark, B. W. 1969b. Aging cells and structures. Int. Audiol. 8(2–3):191–198.

Konigsmark, B. W., and E. A. Murphy. 1972. Volume of the ventral cochlear nucleus in man: Its relationship to neuronal population and age. J. Neuropathol. Exp. Neurol. 31:304–316.

Konkle, D., D. Beasley, and F. Bess. 1977. Intelligibility of time-altered speech in relation to chronological aging. J. Speech Hear. Res. 20:108–115.

Korsan-Bengsten, M. 1973. Distorted speech audiometry. Acta Otolaryngol. (suppl. 310). 75 pp.

Kreul, E., J. Nixon, K. Kryter, D. Bell, J. Lang, and E. Schubert. 1968. A proposed clinical test of speech discrimination. J. Speech Hear. Res. 11:536–552.

Kryter, K. D. 1970. The Effects of Noise on Man. Academic Press, New York.

Landau, W. M., R. Goldstein, and F. R. Kleffner. 1960. Congenital aphasia: A clinicopathologic study. Neurology 10:915–921.

Lansing, R. W., E. Schwartz, and D. B. Lindley. 1959. Reaction time and E.E.G. activation under alerted and nonalerted conditions. J. Exp. Psychol. 58:1–7.

Lawrence, M. 1958. Audiometric manifestations of inner ear physiology: The aural overload test. Transl. Am. Ophthalmol. Otolaryngol. 62:104–119.

Lawrence, M., and C. L. Blanchard. 1954. Prediction of susceptibility to acoustic trauma by determination of threshold of distortion. Industr. Med. Surg. 23: 193–200.

Lawrence, M., and P. A. Yantis. 1956. Onset and growth of aural harmonics in the overloaded ear. J. Acoust. Soc. Am. 28:852–858.

Levitt, H., C. Mayer, and M. Bergman. 1975. Criteria for ambient-noise zone quality standards. Final Report to the New York City Department of Air Resources, Noise Abatement Bureau.

Liberman, A. M. 1957. Some results of research on speech perception. J. Acoust. Soc. Am. 29:117–123.

Licklider, J. C. R., and G. A. Miller. 1951. The perception of speech. In S. S. Stevens (ed.), Handbook of Experimental Psychology. John Wiley & Sons, New York.

Lieberman, M. A. 1969. Institutionalization of the aged: Effects on behavior. J. Gerontol. 24:330–340.

Lipscomb, D. M. 1975. What is the audiogram really telling us? I. Audiometric cochlear damage. Maico Audiol. Libr. Ser. 13(5).

Lotz, J. 1961. The nature and function of language. In S. Saporta (ed.), Psycholinguistics. Holt, Rinehart & Winston, Inc., New York.

Luria, A. R. 1964/1965. Neuropsychology in the local diagnosis of brain damage. Cortex 1:3–18.

Luria, A. R. 1970. The Functional Organization of the Brain. Sci. Am. March: 66–78.

Luria, A. R. 1973. The Working Brain. Basic Books, New York.

Luterman, D., O. Welsh, and J. Melrose. 1966. Responses of aged males to time-altered speech stimuli. J. Speech Hear. Res. 9:226–230.

Lynn, G. E., and J. Gilroy. 1977. Evaluation of central auditory dysfunction in patients with neurological disorders. In R. W. Keith (ed.), Central Auditory Dysfunction. Grune & Stratton, New York.

Mackworth, N. H. 1948. The breakdown of vigilance during prolonged visual search. Quart. J. Exp. Psychol. 10:6–21.

Mackworth, N. H. 1957. Some factors affecting vigilance. Adv. Sci. 13:398–393.

Marsh, G. R., and L. W. Thompson. 1977. Psychophysiology of aging. In J. E. Birren and K. W. Schaie (eds.), Handbook of the Psychology of Aging. Van Nostrand Reinhold Co., New York.

Mayer, C. 1975. The Perception of Speech in Noise as a Function of Age. Doctoral dissertation. City University of New York, New York.

Mehler, J. 1963. Some effects of grammatical transformations on the recall of English sentences. J. Verb. Learn. Behav. 2:346–351.

Miles, W. R. 1942. Psychological aspects of aging. In E. V. Cowdry (ed.), Problems of Aging. The Williams & Wilkins Co., Baltimore.

Miller, G. A. 1947. The masking of speech. Psychol. Bull. 44:105–129.

Miller, G. A. 1951. Language and Communication. McGraw-Hill Book Co., New York.

Miller, G. A. 1956. The magical number 7, plus or minus 2: Some limits on our capacity of processing information. Psychol. Rev. 63:81–97.

Miller, G. A., G. A. Heise, and W. Lichten. 1951. The intelligibility of speech as a function of the context of the test materials. J. Exp. Psychol. 41:329–335.

Miller, G. A., and J. C. R. Licklider. 1950. The intelligibility of interrupted speech. J. Acoust. Soc. Am. 22:167–173.

Miller, G. A., and J. A. Selfridge. 1950. Verbal context and the recall of meaningful material. Am. J. Psychol. 63:176–185.

Milne, J. S. 1977. A longitudinal study of hearing loss in older people. Br. J. Audiol. 11(1):7–14.

Mitchell, P. D. 1973. A Test of Differentiation of Phonemic Feature Contrast. Doctoral dissertation. City University of New York, New York.

Molfese, D. L., R. B. Freeman, Jr., and D. S. Palermo. 1975. The ontogeny of brain lateralization for speech and nonspeech stimuli. Brain Lang. 2:356–368.

Moncur, J. P., and D. Dirks. 1967. Binaural and monaural speech intelligibility in reverberation. J. Speech Hear. Res. 10:186–195.

Nábělek, A. K., and J. M. Pickett. 1974a. Reception of consonants in a classroom as affected by monaural and binaural listening, noise, reverberation and hearing aids. J. Acoust. Soc. Am. 56:628–639.

Nábělek, A. K., and J. M. Pickett. 1974b. Monaural and binaural speech perception through hearing aids under noise and reverberation with normal and hearing impaired listeners. J. Speech Hear. Res. 17:724–739.

National Center for Health Statistics. 1967. Hearing levels of adults by race, region and area of residence, United States: 1960–1962. USPHS Pub. No. 1000, Series 11, No. 26. Government Printing Office, Washington, D.C.

Nikam, S., D. Beasley, and W. Rintelmann. 1976. Perception of time-compressed consonant-nucleus-consonant monosyllables by non-native speaker/listeners of English. J. Am. Audiol. Soc. 2:45–48.

Orgass, B., and K. Poeck. 1966. Clinical validation of a new test for aphasia—An experimental study on the token test. Cortex 2:222–243.

Otomo, E. 1966. Electroencephalography and Clinical Neuro-physiology. Elsevier/North Holland Biomedical Press, Amsterdam.

Penfield, W., and L. Roberts. 1959. Speech and Brain-Mechanisms. Princeton University Press, Princeton, N.J.

Pestalozza, G., and I. Shore. 1955. Clinical evaluation of presbycusis on the basis of different tests of auditory function. Laryngoscope 65:1136–1163.

Peterson, L. R. 1966. Short-term memory. Sci. Am. July:90–95.

Pierce, J. R. 1969. Whither speech recognition? J. Acoust. Soc. Am. 46:1049–1051.

Pierce, J. R., and E. E. David. 1958. Man's World of Sound. Doubleday & Co., Garden City, N.Y.

Post, R. H. 1964. Hearing acuity variation among Negroes and Whites. Eugen. Quart. 11:65–81.

Punch, J. L., and F. McConnell. 1969. The speech discrimination function of elderly adults. J. Aud. Res. 9:159–166.

Rabbitt, P. M. A. 1968. Age and the use of structure in transmitted information. In G. A. Talland (ed.), Human Aging and Behavior. Academic Press, New York.

Randolph, D. 1964. This is Music. Mentor Books, New York.

Reynaud, J., M. Camara, and L. Basteria. 1969. An investigation into presbycusis in Africans from rural and nomadic environments. Int. Audiol. 8(2–3):299–304.

Riegel, K. F. 1968. Changes in psycholinguistic performances with age. In G. A. Talland (ed.), Human Aging and Behavior. Academic Press, New York.

Riegel, K. F. 1977. History of psychological gerontology. In J. E. Birren and K. W. Schaie (eds.), Handbook of the Psychology of Aging. Van Nostrand Reinhold Co., New York.

Roberts, L. 1966. Central brain mechanisms in speech. In E. C. Carterette (ed.), Brain Function, Vol. 3: Speech, Language and Communication. University of California Press, Los Angeles.

Rosen, S., M. Bergman, D. Plester, A. El-Mofty, and M. H. Satti. 1962. Presbycusis study of a relatively noise-free population in the Sudan. Ann. Otol. Rhinol. Laryngol. 71:727–742.

Rosen, S., and P. Olin. 1965. Hearing loss and coronary heart disease. Arch. Otolaryngol. 82:236–243.

Rosenblith, W. A. 1969. Introductory address, Noise as a Public Health Hazard. ASHA Rep. 4:12–17.

Sach, J. S. 1967. Recognition for syntactic and semantic aspects of connected discourse. Percept. Psychophys. 2:437–442.

Samorajski, T. 1976. How the human brain responds to aging. J. Am. Geriatr. Soc. 24:4–11.

Schaie, K. W. 1975. Age changes in adult intelligence. In D. S. Woodruff and J. E. Birren (eds.), Aging: Scientific Perspectives and Social Issues. Van Nostrand Reinhold Co., New York.

Schaie, K. W. 1977. Quasi-experimental research designs in the psychology of aging. In J. E. Birren and K. W. Schaie (eds.), Handbook of the Psychology of Aging. Van Nostrand Reinhold Co., New York.

Schubert, K. 1958. Sprachhörprüfmethoden. Grundlagen, Wurdigung und Anwendung bei Begutachtung and Hörgeräteanpassung. [Speech hearing testing methods. Bases, Evaluation, and Application in Hearing Aid Selection.] Thieme, Stuttgart, Germany.

Schuknecht, H. 1955. Presbycusis. Laryngoscope 65:402–419.

Schuknecht, H. 1964. Further observations on the pathology of presbycusis. Arch. Otolaryngol. 80:369–382.

Schuknecht, H., and M. Igarashi. 1964. Pathology of slowly progressive sensorineural deafness. Transl. Am. Acad. Ophthalmol. Otolaryngol. 68:222–242.

Shankweiler, D., and M. Studdert-Kennedy. 1967. Identification of consonants and vowels presented to left and right ears. Q. J. Exp. Psychol. 19:59–63.

Shock, N. W. 1962. Physiology of aging. Sci. Am. January: 100–110.

Shock, N. W. 1977. Biological theories of aging. In J. E. Birren and K. W. Schaie (eds.), Handbook of the Psychology of Aging. Van Nostrand Reinhold Co., New York.

Siegenthaler, B. 1961. Reaction time, difference limen and amplitude of excursion on normal Békésy audiogram. J. Aud. Res. 1:285–293.

Silverman, I. 1963. Age and the tendency to withold response. J. Gerontol. 17: 372–375.

Slobin, D. 1971. Developmental psycholinguistics. In W. O. Dingwall (ed.), A Survey of Linguistic Science. Linguistic Program, University of Maryland, College Park.

Smith, R., and W. Prather. 1971. Phoneme discrimination in older persons under varying signal-to-noise conditions. J. Speech Hear. Res. 14:630–638.

Smith, B. H., and P. K. Sethi. 1975. Aging and the nervous system. Geriatrics 30: 109–115.

Sohmer, H., and M. Feinmesser. 1973. Routine use of electrocochleography (cochlear audiometry) on human subjects. Audiology 12:167–173.

Spoor, A. 1967. Presbycusis values in relation to noise induced hearing loss. Int. Audiol. 6:48–57.

Steinberg, J. C., H. C. Montgomery, and M. B. Gardner. 1940. Results of the World's Fair hearing tests. J. Acoust. Soc. Am. 12:291–301.

Stevens, K. N., and A. S. House. 1972. Speech perception. In J. Tobias (ed.), Foundations of Modern Auditory Theory, Vol. 2. Academic Press, New York.

Stevens, S. S. (ed.). 1951. Handbook of Experimental Psychology. John Wiley & Sons, New York.

Stevens, S. S., and F. Warshofsky. 1965. Sound and Hearing. LIFE Science Library, p. 31. Time Incorporated, New York.

Sticht, R., and B. Gray. 1969. The intelligibility of time compressed words as a function of age and hearing loss. J. Speech Hear. Res. 12:443–448.

Surwillo, W. 1961. Frequency, the (alpha) rhythm, reaction time, and age. Nature 191:823–824.

Surwillo, W. 1963. The relation of simple response time to brain-wave frequency and the effects of age. EEG Clin. Neurophysiol. 15:105–114.

Surwillo, W., and R. Quilter. 1964. Vigilance, age and response-time. Am. J. Psychol. 77:614–620.

Talland, G. A. (ed.). 1968. Human Aging and Behavior. Academic Press, New York.

Thaler, S., P. Fass, and D. Fitzpatrick. 1973. Marihuana and hearing. Can. J. Otolaryngol. 2(4):291–295.

Thompson, L. W., E. Opton, Jr., and L. D. Cohen. 1963. Effects of age, presentation speed and sensory modality on performance of a "vigilance" task. J. Gerontol. 18:366–369.

Tillman, T. W., and R. Carhart. 1966. An expanded test for speech discrimination utilizing CNC monosyllabic words. Northwestern University Auditory Test No. 6, USAF School of Aerospace Medicine, June.

Timiras, P. S., and A. Vernadakis. 1972. Structural, biochemical and functional aging of the nervous system. In P. S. Timiras (ed.), Developmental Physiology and Aging. Macmillan Publishing Co., New York.

Toyoda, K., and G. Yoshisuke. 1969. Speech discrimination in presbycusis. Int. Audiol. 12:135–139.

Van der Sandt, W., A. Glorig, and R. Dickson. 1969. A survey of the acuity of hearing in the Kalahari Bushman, 1969. Int. Audiol. 8(2–3):290–298.

Wallace, J. G. 1956. Some studies of perception in relation to age. Br. J. Psychol. 47:283–297.

Walsh, D. A. 1975. Age differences in learning and memory. In D. S. Woodruff and J. E. Birren (eds.), Aging: Scientific Perspectives and Social Issues. Van Nostrand Reinhold Co., New York.

Wang, H. S., and E. W. Busse. 1969. EEG of healthy old persons—A longitudinal study: I. Dominant background activity and occipital rhythm. J. Gerontol. 24:419–426.

Warren, R. M. 1970. Perceptual restoration of missing speech sounds. Science 167:392–393.

Webster, J. C., H. W. Himes, and M. Lichtenstein. 1950. San Diego County Fair hearing survey. J. Acoust. Soc. Am. 22:473–483.

Weinberg, J. 1972. Some dynamic aspects of agedness. In C. M. Gaetz (ed.), Advances in Behavioral Biology, Vol. 3. Plenum Press, New York.

Witkin, B. R. 1969. Auditory perception—Implications for language development. J. Res. Dev. Educ. 3(1):53–71.

Wood, N. E. 1971. Auditory perception in children. Final report. Social and Rehabilitation Service Research Grant RD-2574-S. DHEW, Washington, D.C.

Woodruff, D. S. 1975. A physiological perspective of the psychology of aging. In D. S. Woodruff and J. E. Birren (eds.), Aging: Scientific Perspectives and Social Issues. Van Nostrand Reinhold Co., New York.

Woodruff, D. S., and J. E. Birren (eds.). 1975. Aging: Scientific Perspectives and Social Issues. Van Nostrand Reinhold Co., New York.

Zwaardemaker, H. 1899. Der Verlust am Hohen Tonen mit zunehmenden Alter; ein Neues Gesetz. [The loss of high tones with increasing age; a new law.] Arch. Ohrenh. 47.

Author Index

Subject Index